Ray Stevens' Nashville

By Ray Stevens

with C. W. "Buddy" Kalb

Clyde Publishing
A Division of Clyde Records, Inc.
1707 Grand Avenue
Nashville, Tennessee 37212

ISBN: 978-0-578-13886-2

Cover Design:
Ray Stevens

Editor:
Don Cusic

Production Coordinator:
Jim Sharp
Sharp Management

Interior Layout Design:
www.PricelessDigitalMedia.com

Dedication

*To my family, friends, and fans who have made
my life an adventure beyond anything
I could have ever imagined.*

Acknowledgements

*Don Cusic and Buddy Kalb for helping me
assemble my thoughts, memories, and experiences
into something resembling a book.*

Table of Contents

Introduction

In January, 2004, I turned 65 years old. Now, if you live in Georgia or Tennessee and turn 65 it is almost a requirement that you move to Florida or the Gulf Coast, buy some silly hats and shorts, play golf, walk the beach and try to catch the two-for-one early bird specials at the Red Lobster a couple of times each week. My assistant, Shirley Welch, was getting tired of the grind and wanted some time off. I was cutting way back on my performing and falling prey to the idea that I should at least gear down if not pull off the road completely.

In 2002 we told my fan club that I was going to be performing less and recording more and, at that time, I cut office hours back to four days a week. We were doing less. My right hand man, Buddy Kalb, who oversaw our operations, moved to Anna Maria Island in Florida and was coming back and forth as projects required. I had a beach house at Gulf Shores, Alabama – better known on Music Row as L.A. for "Lower Alabama" – but a series of hurricanes caused me to be in constant rebuilding mode down there and not in a relaxed retirement.

In show business, and especially the recording business, people begin to give you the "go away" message as early as age 50, but I had survived for 15 years past that. Many of my contemporary's careers were so cold you could store your beer next to them, but I still received a significant amount of early morning and afternoon drive time radio airplay of my comedy records. But radio was changing. Talk radio was The Big Thing. I used to listen to the Pop and Country stations but discovered that I rarely tuned in to those stations anymore and everybody I knew listened to their CDs, MP3s, iPods or Rush Limbaugh and other talk show hosts.

The heyday of radio and records had passed for me so I began to succumb to the conventional wisdom and let things wind down. There was Shirley and Sherri Puckett and me in the office and we were there only four days a week; we even considered making that a three day week. Then one morning I woke up and said to myself "What am I thinking? I am at the absolute peak of my ability to produce recordings. I have never played or sung better in my life and all I really want to do is make records. So why am I retiring?" I realized that even if I won the lottery, the only thing I wanted to do was make records until all that money was gone.

The most difficult thing about writing is the creative part. There is a craft to writing hit songs, but until there is inspiration, there is no need to apply the craft. I realized that what I cared about was my country. We had been attacked on 9/11 and our troops were in harm's way. Larry McCoy, my bass player at the time, brought me an idea and we wrote the song, "Thank You." It was a 'thank you' to our troops and a reaction against the anti-war, anti-Bush sentiment that had spilled over into the United States Senate, where Senators compared our troops to Nazis on the Senate floor. That fired me up. As Merle Haggard famously wrote during another anti-war period, "When you're puttin' down this country, man, you're walkin' on the fightin' side of me." I found a wealth of inspiration.

The response to "Thank You" at the few concerts I did brought people to their feet. Then I recorded "Safe at Home," a song written by Nick Sibley in Springfield, Missouri, that compared our desire to be safe in our own homes to when we were kids and played baseball games in Grandma's yard. We had lost our sense of security. The crowds loved that one, too. People say you should not discuss religion and politics in show business because it's the kiss of death to a career, so when I began to "get political" with my music I was questioned about that. "Don't you think it's a bad career move?" I was asked. I replied,

"When you are over 65, there are no bad career moves." In show business, I had been there, done that, had a wonderful life and career and was fortunate enough to not have to work another day in my life. If I wanted to do something, then why shouldn't I do it? Isn't that what retirement is all about, doing what you want to do?

My fans responded positively to my expressions of patriotism. I had genuine concerns about the direction our country was headed, especially after the election of President Barack Obama. Liberals in show business have no problem lacing their comedy routines with their point of view or writing their progressive opinions into movie scripts so I decided to join the conservative voices of Bruce Willis, Charlie Daniels, Jon Voight, Gary Sinise and a few others and be conservative publically like I had always been privately.

Buddy Kalb shares my political views and began to write in that conservative political direction, which led me to record my sentiments and political opinions. I was going to produce a standard length album, but after I started, the songs began to pour out.

So how does an aging recording artist with 'too hot to handle' music get it heard? The gate keepers at radio and TV will allow you only limited access, but there are a few exceptions: talk radio, the Fox News Channel, and the internet. We didn't ignore regular radio or TV, but we didn't count on them, either. We focused on those three outlets, beginning with the internet.

We studied what was happening on the web. Music was being stolen because the generation that grew up with Napster believes music should be free. They pride themselves on their ability to find music and share it with all their friends without paying. Either they have no idea, or they don't care about what is involved in creating and producing a recording.

We closely examined the playing field and decided that if people think our music should be free, then we'll give it to them. Isn't that what we did with radio for years? Our records were played by radio for listening audiences while artists and record companies were not paid for that "promotion" in the hope that listeners liked a song enough to want to own it. That model still worked; however, the problem now was that ownership of a recording could be acquired at no cost by many of the listeners. Still, some wanted a physical product they could hold in their hand and some still felt it was wrong to take something for nothing. So we had to direct our efforts toward those people and not get too distracted by music thieves.

We created an internet video and discovered that on sites like YouTube there are a large number of viewers who are attracted to cheap, sometimes cheesy videos. The most popular ones were musical and the most popular of those were funny, so we began to write songs that were hopefully poignant as well as funny. We wanted to make serious points with humor. A spoonful of sugar always helps the medicine go down, as Mary Poppins used to say.

Then we realized that those who watch YouTube are usually seated at a desk and are accustomed to someone on the screen being right in their face, like a news anchor. That led us to produce close shots in bright colors. We did that economically by using green screen technology and putting in the backgrounds after shooting my part. I used the track of music from the record and lip-synced the words. I own a TV production studio with a large green screen and editing equipment. We hired Doug Phillips, a young editor and internet specialist who had recently graduated from Belmont University here on Music Row. Doug could shoot a video one day and edit it the next. Once we had the music track, we could be on YouTube in a couple of days.

As of this writing, the Ray Stevens videos on YouTube have attracted over 60 million unique views. A "unique" view is one view per computer for each video; multiple views from the same computer are not counted, only the initial view. That means that 60 million 'unique' views could amount to as many as 240 million actual views or even more. And those are only the YouTube views! The videos get picked up by other websites and added to their front pages because the web owner agrees with the political sentiment expressed. So, the messages I believe in are being shared around the web and around the world, and since we always imbed "www.raystevens.com" at the bottom of every video, we get lots of traffic to our website. There, people can get stuff for free if they give us their e-mail address and permission to send them an e-mail from time to time, or they can own any of my CD or DVD products or download them for a small price.

We sell our products via iTunes, Amazon, and other web sales outlets. The YouTube exposure stimulates radio and TV interest, which leads me to do interviews on national radio shows and cable TV news outlets. Bill O'Reilly and his staff at Fox News Channel have been supportive of my comedic approach on conservative political issues and have shown several of our videos on his show where he has invited me to appear from time to time. I have also appeared on the shows of Sean Hannity, Judge Andrew Napolitano, Mike Huckabee, David Asmon, Fox and Friends, Megyn Kelly, and others.

So here I am, an over-the-hill recording artist in his early 70s with resurgence in my career in a direction that people warned me not to go. It's not the first time. Early on I was told, "Don't do comedy – it's a fast burn" and then someone said "It's a waste of time to try to sell videos to anyone, they are only for promotional purposes, nobody will want to own one." Then I heard, "If you sell stuff on TV, that's the kiss of death and a sure sign your career is over." Then there was, "The internet is a waste of time. All you'll do is give away your whole catalog for free." And the latest warning, "Don't let people know your political beliefs because it will turn off half of your audience." They fail to realize that it will really energize the other half. But in my case, the turn-off group has amounted to less than 5%, and the 95% who share my opinions have responded with enthusiasm.

Now, here's a really good word of advice: Never say "No" to yourself. You can always count on somebody else to do that.

So what's next? Well I'm Tweeting and Facebooking and YouTubing and social networking and e-mail blasting like crazy and I'll keep doing my political songs and videos as long as I feel I can make a difference. I've got lots of new projects in the works and I guess I always will.

This is where I am today, but as they used to say on one of my favorite radio shows when I was a kid "Let me take you back to those thrilling days of yester-year." Let me share where I came from and how I got to this point. First, you will need a little perspective.

CHAPTER 1

A Little Overview

Everyone born in a mill town in rural Georgia in 1939, had a few solid pillars in their life. There was family, church, baseball and the radio.

It may seem strange to mention baseball as a pillar of life, but this was before TV and air-conditioned anything, except the occasional movie theatre, and baseball really was The National Pastime. My dad owed his job at the mill to the fact that he was a good baseball player and helped the Coats and Clark team win a lot of games. I loved baseball and wanted to play like my Dad. The mill community was at the ball park regularly through the spring, summer and early fall to watch him and his friends play.

On the radio, we listened to what we considered Big League baseball when they broadcast games of the Atlanta Crackers as they played teams like the Birmingham Barons, Memphis Chicks, Chattanooga Lookouts and Nashville Vols. The radio also brought us the WSB Barn Dance from Atlanta and the show of all radio shows, The Grand Ole Opry, from WSM in Nashville, Tennessee.

Later, I listened to WLAC in Nashville where Randy's Record Shop sponsored Rhythm and Blues shows with disc jockeys like The Hoss Man (Hoss Allen) and John R. (John Richbourg). Rhythm and Blues, or R&B, caught my attention when I was a young teenager.

Nashville was miles and miles away, somewhere up Highway 41 north of Chattanooga and past Monteagle. It was where musicians and singers like Hank Williams, Pee Wee King, Eddy Arnold and Red Foley lived and worked. It was where Chet Atkins played guitar like there were two or three pickers playing, but it was just him – one man with two hands on a guitar – that sounded like the whole band. It was Hillbilly Hollywood.

I first became involved in the music business in Atlanta, but I went to Nashville to work on recording sessions with other young musicians from Atlanta from time to time. That's how I became familiar with that route over Monteagle and back. I remember the "See Rock City" signs painted on barns, the Stuckey's stops, and Burma Shave signs. They were all on that winding, two-lane, black-top road that carried us to Nashville.

It was not until 1962, at the ripe old age of 23, that I moved to Nashville after I was offered a job by Shelby Singleton, the head of Mercury Records' Nashville operations as an assistant A&R man for Mercury. That's when I loaded up all of my possessions, which only took up about half the room in a small U-Haul trailer, and drove my wife and young baby up Route 41 from Atlanta to Nashville. When I did that, my relationship with Nashville changed. As I crossed the Davidson County line, just north of Murfreesboro, I did not consciously realize it, but I was home.

Nashville has been my home for over fifty years. When I first came to this city, Music Row was not fully developed and the music business was mostly in the downtown area. There was no "Nashville Sound" per se, no major league teams or interstate highways, and no Opryland. The recording studios and publishing offices were scattered around town and as far away as Hendersonville, about twenty miles north of the city.

Over the years, the major record labels made major investments in buildings, staffs, and offices. A support industry of booking agents, studio equipment suppliers, duplication facilities, and music business lawyers settled here. Belmont, a local university, began to offer courses for young students in the music business. The business changed from pressing vinyl discs to duplicating 8-tracks and then cassettes and from analog to digital with CDs and DVDs. Music Row grew as the music industry centralized there. Musicians kept making the best music they could and let the engineers and technicians figure out the delivery systems. Little by little, as I worked here, watched and made my contributions to the world of music, my adopted hometown became Nashville – Music City.

I want to tell you all about that process and about Nashville – 'My Nashville.' But for me, before Nashville and Music City, there was Clarkdale, Georgia.

CHAPTER 2

Clarkdale

I was born in Clarkdale, Georgia, population 550. It was 550 on January 24, 1939, and it's still 550 today. I think every time a baby is born somebody must leave town. At the beginning of 1939, the world was temporarily at peace but on the verge of the Second World War. Adolph Hitler had not yet invaded Poland – that happened on September 1 – nor had a single bomb fallen on London, while Pearl Harbor was a little known port in the Pacific where the United States Navy docked their ships. Hank Williams was a teenager, playing his guitar and singing on a 15-minute radio show in Montgomery, Alabama, while in Tupelo, Mississippi, a four-year-old barefoot boy named Elvis Aron Presley lived with his parents in a three room "shotgun" house. In 1939, no one had ever heard the term rock'n'roll.

During the following year, the United States instituted the draft for young men and began to mobilize for War. Just north of Atlanta, a large bomber plant was built for the war effort. As the world confronted War in Europe and the possibility that it might even come to the shores of the United States, life in the mill town of Clarkdale, Georgia, 25 miles west of Atlanta, hardly missed an idyllic beat.

Clarkdale grew up around the Clark Thread Company, which built the town in 1932. (Later, Clark Thread merged with J & P Coats to form Coats and Clark Thread Company.) Since textiles were vital to the war effort, most of the men who worked in the textile industry were exempt from military service. During 1940 and 1941, it was difficult to import or export anything because German U-Boats roamed the Atlantic, sinking ships. Over in the Pacific Ocean, a powder keg exploded when the Japanese bombed Pearl Harbor on Sunday, December 7, 1941, and the United States entered the War with all we had.

Willis Harold and Frances Stephens Ragsdale were married and employed at the mill, living far from the chaos of war. They met their needs from steady jobs at the mill, which provided more than a paycheck. They lived in a house built by the mill, shopped at a local general store nearby, and found recreation among like-minded, good-hearted, hard-working people who shared their fortunate fate. I'm not sure what my Daddy's job was at the mill during those days, but the real reason he was employed was because of his ability to hit the cover off of a baseball and cover third base like a cat. Dad was a power hitter and wore a uniform with pin stripes, like the New York Yankees, with "Clarkdale" in big letters across the front of his shirt.

Baseball was important; the mill's reputation in the community was tied to the performance of their baseball team. In those days every company, church and civic organization had a team. Baseball wasn't just a sport, it was truly the national pastime. We worked, went to school, went to church on Sundays and Wednesday evenings, but we spent more time hanging around the baseball field than any other place. My Dad and his friends, like 'Bully' Coalson, were stars and local heroes and I wanted to be a baseball player just like them when I grew up. Bully and Dad were the fearsome bats on the Coats and Clark team. With Daddy at third, Bully behind the plate, and J.B. Williams on the pitcher's mound, most of the teams in that part of Georgia were seriously outclassed. My Dad's team proved Leo Durocher wrong when he said, "Nice guys finish last," because these were some of the nicest guys I knew and they almost always finished first.

All the kids played baseball on a big grassy hill where the cotton mill sat. Our bases were trees, and we used old broken bats that we had glued and taped together. I played when I was little but I was not as good as my Dad, and never played organized baseball.

To say that my Dad was the strong silent type would be a gross understatement because he hardly spoke at all. His Daddy was the sheriff of Paulding County, and he made my Daddy look like a gossiping gab-bag. Those two would sit on the front porch together for hours sipping iced tea and never say a word.

My Dad was very independent and self-sufficient. He didn't look for or expect anyone to take care of him; Dad didn't much care for President Franklin Roosevelt and his New Deal, either. He thought Social Security and all Government Entitlement programs were a crock – and so do I. He was always a straight-down-the-line conservative. He grew up on a farm and his Dad was a butcher who owned land in Paulding County and became a pillar of that community. When my Dad was just a kid, he hitched up a team of mules and plowed. If somebody does that when they're a kid, they're pretty healthy and don't really need to depend on anyone else.

My grandfather was a sheriff and owned a general store where people came to get their corn ground into meal. He also had a sugar cane patch and grew sugar cane. Once a year they'd build a big fire, hitch the mules to a big stone wheel, feed the cane in, and the juice came out. Then they'd boil that juice into a big pot and make sorghum syrup. Ever had sorghum syrup with a glob of butter mashed up in it and then slathered the mixture on a hot biscuit? Oh my!

My mother sure could make biscuits, and was outgoing and vivacious. She loved a joke, arranging flowers, and her boys: Dad, me and John, my little brother, who was born on June 30, 1944. It was fine with her that I loved baseball, but she also wanted me to be a little more cultured and she had hopes for me beyond a Georgia mill town. She insisted on piano lessons when I was six. Mom not only insisted on the lessons, but required at least one hour of practice each and every day.

It was hard to sit and practice piano while the sounds of my friends playing baseball outside drowned out the halting notes I forced from the old upright piano in our home. But Mama insisted that I practice each day – and that's exactly what I did. Little by little, the piano began to actually interest me, and so I applied myself to those practices rather than just enduring the hour. Then, one day as I was practicing the "Marine Hymn," I had an epiphany. I can't explain it, really, but it was as though all of the little grey cells in my brain aligned with the musical cosmos and I sat staring in surprise at the keyboard. The keys, my hand, and my brain all said, "Hey, I see how this works! I get it!"

It struck me like a flash of light that the basic three

notes of a chord were a triad and you can use that triad to make a chord in any key. Middle C is right in the middle and the piano is laid out in a sequence so you can move that chord with those three notes up or down. From that moment on, the piano ceased to be a piece of furniture or even a musical instrument that I was required to do something to. Instead it became an extension of my mind, hands, and fingers. Playing piano was as easy as singing – and I discovered that I could express a song through that keyboard just as easily as I could sing it. The piano became a part of me; it captured me and somehow I knew it would never let me go.

During the war, life in Clarkdale did not change much. The Coats and Clark Mills had a swimming pool where Bonnie Boyd, a pretty blonde life guard, taught me to swim. I've never had a fear of water since. Her daddy was P.T. Boyd, the local constable of sorts. Mr. Boyd had an easy job because there was no need to lock doors or watch your back in Clarkdale. There was zero crime because everyone looked out for everyone else, so a peaceful equality pervaded the whole community. At least that's how it seemed to me. Looking back, I have memories of a wonderful childhood comprised of school, playing with friends, and learning more and more about the piano as I ventured past the sheet music the teacher gave me and into the popular songs I heard on the radio.

Now, radio was another cornerstone of our simple lives and, in those days, there were not a lot of radio stations. There was usually one major station with a powerful signal that attempted to meet the desires of all their listeners. When it came to music, they programmed a wide variety: Big Band, Pop, Country, Gospel, and even the occasional Black or Blues song that was called Race Music in those days. In large metropolitan areas you could find lower power stations that specialized in a specific genre like Gospel or Race but, for the most part, the big stations like WSB in Atlanta carried music based on its general popularity, regardless of its genre. I loved that. You could hear Bing Crosby followed by Roy Acuff followed by Kate Smith and on Saturdays there was opera. Then, on Saturday night, just after an Opera show on WSM, Nashville's 50,000 watt station that blanketed the southeast after the sun went down, the announcer famously said "You've been listening to Grand Opera on WSM and now it's time for the Grand Ole Opry. Let 'er go boys!" and an institution was born. It was the "American Idol" of its day where you heard talented but not formerly educated people sing and play for the entire country. The performer's popularity on that program was based on cards and letters mailed in by listeners after a performance, which led to stardom for many, just like it does today – except that today people can email or tweet their responses instantaneously.

Major radio stations broadcast shows like "The Lone Ranger" and "Gang Busters" or comedy shows like "Amos and Andy" and "George Burns and Gracie Allen" that kept a family laughing together as they sat around their Philco, Crosley, or Zenith radio sets in the living room. Our radio was in the living room of our house, which was a three-room duplex in the mill village. Later, we moved into a five-room house and then an eight-room house in the same place. They were all white clapboard and the roofs were slate. I used to lie on the rug in the living room and listen to the radio. I loved those famous shows and didn't realize there were actual writers who wrote scripts for those voices. I thought they made everything up as they went along.

Musicians got their start back then playing on live radio shows and the recording studios of the era were often part of a radio station. Only in New York or Los Angeles were recording studios separate from radio stations. In Nashville, there was a studio at WSM but that was not yet "my" Nashville. For me, Albany, Georgia, came next.

CHAPTER 3

Albany

I don't remember Pearl Harbor – I was only two when that happened – but I remember when World War II ended in August, 1945. All the cars in Clarkdale were out, blowing their horns as they drove through the streets with girls riding on the hoods of the cars, cheering.

After World War II ended, my Dad received promotions at Coats and Clark for his abilities inside the plant as well as on the baseball diamond. His first promotion meant a transfer to their facility in Albany in Southwest Georgia. Down there the town is pronounced *ALL-Benny*. I was ten and my brother John was five and that move was a big adventure. Daddy bought a new Buick and we made that long hot drive to South Georgia full of anticipation; I was excited about the move and I was not disappointed.

Those seven years I spent growing up in Albany produced some of the fondest memories of my life. My Dad built a house that was bigger and nicer than the one in Clarkdale. As I matured from a young boy to a young man, the social opportunities were plentiful. I especially remember the summers, which seemed to last all year in South Georgia. Radium Springs was a beautiful artesian spring that offered swimming and a family picnic area that was a mecca for kids. I can still remember the thrill of diving into that cold, crystal clear spring on a hot South Georgia day. I also vividly remember my days in the school band; I wanted to play every instrument, and the band director allowed me the opportunity.

I started out on clarinet, then tried baritone, trumpet, drums, and even tuba. I loved music and wanted to learn everything about it. It was in Albany where I first became known, and thought of myself, as a musician. It wasn't long before I wanted to form my own band. So, with class-mates Bob Duggleby on trumpet, Bill Garrison on sax, and Terry Coleman on drums, joining me at the piano, "The Barons" were born. Terry's brother was Don Coleman, a great sax player and they had a band, The Stardusters, who played for big time dances at the American Legion, the Elks Club, and places like that.

The Barons practiced at my house. We made a list of songs and rehearsed and then word somehow got out and people called. We played for $150 a night. We were popular in school and played a lot of dances and other functions at school and in the community. That was my first foray into the world of playing in a band, arranging, and singing, the things that defined my life for years to come. At that time I was just having fun, but it was all working together to prepare me for a career that I couldn't even imagine back then.

I earned money playing those gigs, so with $750 in my pocket I went to Atlanta with my Dad where, on a used car lot near the Varsity Drive-in, I bought my first car: it was a 1952 Mercury. What a piece of junk! It had a chrome air scoop on the hood. I kept the air scoop but I got rid of the rest of the chrome and painted it black. They used to call that "shaved" when you took off all the chrome. My favorite part of that car was the radio. I loved the simplicity of having just two knobs – one turned the radio on and off and controlled the volume, while you turned the other knob to find stations. I loved to find stations when I was in the car.

I was a popular guy with a band and my own car and I was having the time of my life. My reputation as a musician and popular guy around town led Milton George, the manager of WGPC, the local radio station (the call letters stood for "Worlds Greatest Pecan Center") to offer me a job as a disc jockey on a Saturday afternoon show playing records for kids my age. Milt told me that if I found a girl to co-host he would put us on the air for the Saturday afternoon "record hop." I didn't waste a minute; I called

Mary Dale Van Zant and the next week we were broadcasting the latest hits to the kids in Southwest Georgia.

My tastes in music were growing and maturing and I really dug the Rhythm and Blues (R&B) groups of the day, like The Clovers and The Coasters. As the fifties approached their mid-point, the music in America blossomed. Ray Charles, who also started life near Albany, was on Atlantic Records, Elvis Presley was on Sun Records in Memphis, and Little Richard Penniman from Macon, Georgia, were all grabbing the attention of kids in America. Lightning was striking all around me as I began to dream of a Rock'n'Roll career. I didn't want to just perform the hits of others at high school sock hops, I wanted to play my own hits for audiences all over the world. The realization of that dream was way out on the horizon, but it kept getting closer.

When my Dad was awarded his next promotion at Coats and Clark, I was finishing my junior year of high school in Albany. That promotion meant another transfer, this time to Atlanta. I was heartbroken. Here I was, soon to be a cool high school senior, the zenith of my school experience, and I had to give up all that and move to a different school full of strangers whose relationships were all well established. I was going from being a Big Shot Somebody to a No Shot Nobody at the most crucial time in my young life. It felt like the world was caving in.

We moved to the Druid Hills section of Atlanta in 1956, and I started my senior year in a new high school. I did not realize it at the time, but that big lemon I'd been given was going to turn into a giant pitcher of lemonade and my heartbreak was going to turn into my Big Break.

Radio and jukeboxes were playing the fire out of Elvis and other young Rock'n'Roll performers, but there was something else in people's homes now: a television. By 1956, people were eating TV dinners while watching the programs in black and white on their TV set, which had replaced the radio as the center of home entertainment. I believe my Dad bought the first TV set in town. It was not very big and I used to watch the test pattern (which had an Indian with a full headdress) for hours. However, radio had not completely died; it was alive and well on the dashboards of almost every car in America that was cruising the streets.

All of that was a bright light I didn't see during my personal dark time as I traveled with my family from Albany, where I was on top of the world, to Atlanta, where I was sure I'd be in a deep valley of despair.

CHAPTER 4

Atlanta: The New Kid in Town

Moving to Atlanta induced a Culture Shock! There was a big difference in that big city compared to Albany in 1956. Druid Hills High School, near the Emory University campus, was not like Albany High school and there was no mill community like I'd been used to. We lived in the sprawling suburbs of a major growing city, but the one constant was music. Rhythm and Blues was big in Atlanta because WAOK was devoted to it. Thirteen Eighty-O on the Ray-dio was run by Zenas Sears, who owned the station and played records. His other DJs included "The Dream Girl" Zilla Mays and Pat Patrick, who called himself "Alley Pat." "Piano Red" was a roadhouse piano playing albino black guy who hosted a show as well as made records. Red always played a lot of Piano Red records – of course – and it helped him make a good living playing gigs around Atlanta. It was a lesson in the power of how radio can make a recording career.

My love of both Pop and R&B music, and my talent as a musician, made the transition from small town to big city easier because music paved the way. My ability to play and sing the popular songs of the day immediately opened doors for me that would have otherwise been shut during my important senior year. Instead of being an outsider, I was instantly accepted and made new friends quickly. There was a high school fraternity/sorority system at Druid Hills. The number one fraternity was Kappa Delta Kappa, or "The KDK's," and the number one sorority were the Sunevs, which is 'Venus' spelled backwards. I was "rushed" and became a KDK during my first weeks at my new high school. I was active in Band and began to focus on trumpet.

When spring break came, most of the kids in Atlanta went to Panama City, Florida. It was not as wild then as it has become, but it was wild enough for me to have my first and only brush with the law. Apart from an occasional speeding ticket, I've always been on friendly terms with The Law. I did get pulled over for speeding the other day and when the officer said he was going to give me a ticket I said, "Aw come on, can't you just let me off with a warning?" So he pulled his gun and fired three shots over my head. I may never speed again. (Actually, this didn't happen, but it just shows how far some people will go to tell a dumb joke.)

Carl Aiken was the president of KDK during the Spring Break of 1957, and I was with him at "The Hangout" in

Panama City where all the kids gathered to dance to the latest songs and hopefully hook up for a teen-age tryst on the beach. As I remember it, there was a whole lot more hoping than hooking up going on. The "Hangout" had several pinball machines and Carl was quite aggressive with his body-English while I stood by watching. In frustration, he suddenly hit the top of the pinball machine and the glass shattered.

The cops were on Carl like ugly on an ape and I was scooped up with him and hauled off to the Bay County Jail where I spent the night in the Drunk Tank. Hey, I wasn't even drunk and hadn't even been drinking. Carl was released. He was not yet 17 and the law let "under-age" first offenders off with a warning. But for me, it was an especially long night, sober and scared and surrounded by a bunch of drunks in a jail cell out of town. It might have been good material for a Johnny Cash song, but I spent that night praying my Mama would not find out about this misadventure, in addition to wishing I was big enough to whip Carl's ass for getting me arrested. However, Carl's ass was attached to a very big ole boy, so I just fumed to myself and stayed awake all night. The next morning, Carl agreed to pay for the pinball machine repair and we were released without charges. So ended my short life on the wrong side of The Law.

In the big sprawling city of Atlanta, there was no close mill community or baseball games where Daddy starred at third base, but family was still strong and church remained a constant. My family regularly attended Clairmont Hills Baptist Church at the corner of Clairmont Road and Briarcliff Road. My Sunday school teacher was Warren Roberts, who was also a Disc Jockey and station manager at WEAS in the neighboring community of Decatur. At church, Warren was aware of my talent and my interests. One day he told me, "You need to meet Bill Lowery." I said, "Who's Bill Lowery" and he said, "Here's his phone number. Call him." I called him on Monday and went over to his house and told him about my band and interest in music and he said, "Fine, lad. Why don't you write me a song."

Backstage at a TV event recently, I was talking to Bill Anderson, who is also from the Atlanta area and also got his musical start there with Bill Lowery, but I didn't realize that Warren Roberts had also been influential in his life as well. It's a small world.

A little factual background on Bill Lowery is in order here. Bill was born in Leesville, Louisiana, in 1924 – so he was 33 when I met him. He had studied to be a radio announcer at Taft Junior College and was a natural with a gift of gab and was a hit wherever he worked. He had worked at radio stations in Louisiana and Tennessee before he made it to the Big Time in Atlanta where his on-air persona was "Uncle Eb Brown."

In 1951, Bill discovered that a small growth on his leg was cancer. The growth was removed and the doctors were pretty certain they had fixed the problem, but no insurance company wanted to take a chance with his pre-existing condition so he couldn't get insurance of any kind for himself or his young family. A disc jockey friend of Bill's, Tex Davis, who was on a radio station in Norfolk, Virginia, encouraged Bill to start a music publishing company – or some other entrepreneurial venture – in order to create income outside his radio station salary to help offset possible future catastrophic expenses. Bill worked for station WEAS in Decatur, Georgia, and then for WGST, the Georgia Tech station, where he called the Georgia Tech ball games. He was very popular and well liked in the greater Atlanta area. He took his friend's advice and began a music publishing company and searched for new songs from young writers all over Atlanta and North Georgia.

The company that Bill started in Atlanta acquired the copyright to "Be Bop A Lula," a huge hit in the summer of 1956 by Gene Vincent, that stayed on the charts for twenty weeks. Gene came from Norfolk and Tex Davis "discovered" him there. Tex was the co-writer of "Be Bop A Lula," and he had his friend Bill Lowery handle the publishing for him. So, here was a brand new publishing company with a huge Rock'n'Roll hit right out of the box. Fortune shined on Bill and many a young wannabe basked in the glow for years to come.

Bill Lowery, this highly successful music publisher, had told me to write a song for him and I wondered, "What can I write about?" Teenage songs were big at that time, 'Bubble Gum' music is what it was called and so I got the idea for "Silver Bracelet." It was a teen-age ditty about a chain link I.D. bracelet that a guy gave a girl (or vice versa) back then with the name of the recipient engraved on front and the name of the giver on the back. It was a very popular piece of jewelry with teens of that era. I called a high school friend of mine, Will Rogers, Jr. (no relation to the famous Will Rogers) who was a word guy, and he helped me put it together. In order to have a good demo or "demonstration record" to present to Mr. Lowery, I decided to use the Druid Hills High School cafeteria, which had an upright piano.

I asked for and received permission from the principal, Mr. McDaniel, to use the cafeteria on a Saturday afternoon. He said, "Sure, here's the key." Can you imagine something like that happening today? Life was much kinder and simpler back then!

I borrowed a cheap reel-to-reel tape recorder from my

friend Richard Cheek, and on Saturday I unlocked the door, went in the school cafeteria, and experimented with positioning the microphone until I found the nice echo sound I wanted. I sat at the piano, which was on the stage, and sang "Silver Bracelet" and the tape captured it. I played back what I had recorded and thought, "Boy, that sounds pretty good!" Then I packed up everything, locked the door, and turned in the key to Mr. McDaniel on Monday morning.

I wish I could tell a long, sad, dramatic story of walking the streets and knocking on door after door for years trying to get someone to listen to my songs. It might make a more interesting book, but the truth is that I took that seven and a half inch reel of tape to Bill Lowery, the first demo of the first song I had ever written to my first publisher – and he loved it.

Bill Lowery was a larger-than-life, heavy set man with big jowls and a head full of long, silver hair that he combed back in an Elvis-like ducktail. He had the enthusiasm of the entire Dallas Cowboys cheerleading squad or a room full of Mary Kay sales ladies all packed into that well groomed and nattily dressed body. As my song played on his tape recorder, Bill shot up from the chair behind his desk and exploded with enthusiasm, "Lad – that's a HIT!" He called his secretary, Mary Talent, to "Come listen to this! Play it again lad! *Play it again!!!!!*"

I had never seen such a reaction from an adult to anything I had done in all my life. No, wait – I'd never seen that kind of reaction from anybody about anything at all, ever. Like I said earlier, my Daddy hardly even spoke. I never imagined a grown man pacing around a room, gesturing wildly and enthusiastically, effusively, about my song. It was not the last time I was to see such a reaction from Bill Lowery because he was a bottomless pit of enthusiasm, an unending spring of encouragement exuding acceptance and confidence. He was a wide-screen, Technicolor, surround-sound version of himself, just like a heroic character from a comic book or a mid-way barker at a carnival show. Every time he spoke it was like sparkling confetti fell from the ceiling and light beamed from his eyes. In short order, I had a record deal. I did not suffer for my art or labor for years in anonymity striving for success. In fact, I still stand amazed by it.

I made my first trip to Nashville in 1957, and recorded "Silver Bracelet" in the RCA Studio, which at that time was located on McGavock Street in the Methodist Radio and Television building. Bill loved the Anita Kerr singers, so he hired them to sing back-up on the record but mixed them up so high that it sounded like an Anita Kerr Singers record. Bill played the recording for Ken Nelson, the head of A&R for Capitol Records, who said, "Bill, you've covered up the singer with the background singers. Let me re-record it." Bill agreed, so once again I went to Nashville, back into that same studio but this time with Ken Nelson producing and mixing the record.

By the time I graduated from Druid Hills High School in June, 1957, "Silver Bracelet" was a regional hit on the Prep label, a new subsidiary of Capitol Records. The reason the term "label" came into being in the industry was because a few record companies controlled a lot of subsidiaries and since all records were black plastic or vinyl with either a big hole or a little one in the center, the only distinguishing mark was the label that was glued around the hole in the center of the disk. That label was unique to the entity that was releasing it and was their trademark. In addition to the label name, there was the title of the song, the artist, the writer/s, publisher, the performing rights organization (like ASCAP or BMI), record number, and the time or length so disc jockeys knew how long the song was.

The name on the record was Ray Stevens, not Ray Ragsdale, because Ken Nelson, the Artist and Repertoire (A&R) executive at Capitol didn't think that Ray Ragsdale had marquee value; it just didn't "pop." I told Ken that my mother would not take very kindly to me or anyone else changing my name so he asked, "What's your mother's maiden name?" I told him "Stephens" and he said that was fine, but even then he changed the spelling from Stephens to Stevens.

CHAPTER 5

Learning the Music Business

"**S**ilver Bracelet" found its way onto several regional charts. It was a genuine teen-age Rock'n'Roll radio hit. I had affirmed my identity as a musician in the bigger pond that was Atlanta, and that Fall I planned to enter college at Georgia Tech to study architecture. However, Bill Lowery told me, "Son, you need to be in the music business" so I enrolled in Georgia State in Atlanta as a music major while my education in the music business came over the next three years at the side of Bill Lowery and NRC, which stood for "National Recording Company," the label Bill started in Atlanta.

Bill not only attracted me, but also several other young musicians who aspired to become recording artists. One of the trademarks of our group is that we all had to change our names. A handsome guitar virtuoso by the name of Jerry Hubbard became Jerry Reed. Another great guitar player and songwriter named Joe Souter became Joe South. And a young guy who became a close friend in years to come, Buddy Kalb, became Big Buddy K.

Prior to opening his own record label and recording studio, Bill would regularly take us to Nashville and rent the Quonset Hut or RCA's new recording studio (later known as "RCA Studio B") for a day so we could all record songs we had written. During those trips, Jerry Reed, Joe South, and I became acquainted with the Nashville pickers and producers who were making hits heard all around the world.

The Nashville recording industry was well established by the time Bill attempted to launch his own version of Nashville in Atlanta. It was not to be the last time that I was in the right place at the right time.

On one of our early trips to Nashville, we recorded The Techniques, a group from Georgia Tech. As we drove to Nashville, Jerry Reed and I stopped at a roadside gas station and store to get gas, and each of us bought a crazy hat. On that session, we were wearing those hats – one was a derby and the other was a top hat – when Chet Atkins stopped by. That was the first time I met Chet; I think he thought we were nuts.

A little factual background on Chet Atkins is in order here.

Around the time my family moved to Albany, a young guitar player who was to have a major impact on my life decided to give up life on the road and settle in Nashville and make his living as a session player. Chester Burton Atkins started out playing on the radio in Knoxville, then moved to Cincinnati, and then travelled on the road playing for Mother Maybelle and the Carter Family before he landed in Nashville for good. The increasing number of country music recordings that were coming out of Nashville caused him to focus on studio work, so he settled there with his wife, Leona, and young daughter, Merle (named for his hero Merle Travis) to play on recording sessions for Steve Sholes, who was in charge of RCA Victor Records in Nashville at that time.

Chet's brother, Jim, had a reputation as an excellent guitarist and worked with Les Paul and others so, not wanting to compete with his brother, Chet started his music career as a fiddle player. He was playing one-nighters with Jumpin' Bill Carlisle and Archie Campbell, going gig to gig with all of them crowded into a Cadillac. One day while traveling, he sat in the back seat playing a tune on a guitar in that distinctive Atkins style that he refined over the years. Bill Carlisle asked, "What's that you're playin' back there?" Chet replied that it was just a song he was working on and Bill asked, "Do you know any other ones?" Chet answered that he knew two or three more, whereupon Bill exclaimed, "Good! You're our new guitar player 'cause you're a *turr-ible* fiddle player."

Around the same time Chet was establishing himself as a studio musician in Nashville, Owen Bradley was building studios here. After having several studios around town, Owen built one in a Army surplus Quonset hut behind a house he bought on 16th Avenue, which became the first studio in the area that was to become known as "Music Row." It was known officially as "The Bradley Recording Studio," but everyone just called it "The Quonset Hut."

During the mid-1950s, as I was maturing in South Georgia, the Nashville music industry had been growing up too. Chet Atkins became known as "Mr. Guitar" with a couple of top selling singles like "Mr. Sandman," and then he took over as head of RCA's Nashville recording operations. Owen Bradley became head of Decca Records and his Quonset Hut Studio became a home for a long run of hits. As a producer, Chet was also recording monster hits on a number of artists at a record pace, and records coming out of both those studios began to reach beyond the country music charts with Patsy Cline's pop-like crossovers and two brothers named Everly who were sensations in every market both here and abroad. Then there was Elvis, whose contract was sold to RCA Victor by Sam Phillips and his Sun Records label in Memphis. After that, Elvis did a lot of recording in Nashville.

The Nashville scene was solidifying by the late 1950s, and Nashville became a major recording center for all types of music. A gospel vocal group who'd been successful as far back as 1950, became the first-call male background singers and their association with Elvis Presley made Gordon Stoker's Jordanaires stars in their own right. Then there was The Anita Kerr Singers who sang on my first recording, who became the top "mixed" group – two ladies and two gents – singing background on numerous sessions.

It seemed like all of the eagles had gathered in Nashville. At first, the publishing and record companies were scattered around town but, little by little, the houses and lots on 16th and 17th Avenues were bought or leased by music industry people, turned into music business-related companies as Music Row took shape. "The boys who made the noise on 16th Avenue" were heard all around the world. But I still had things to learn and dues to pay in Atlanta before I was ready to move to The Big Show in Nashville.

While all of this was happening in Nashville, the music publishing company Bill Lowery started in Atlanta not only owned the copyright to the Rock'n'Roll standard "Be Bop A Lula," but was beginning to make some noise with other songs he published like "Young Love." Bill Lowery was a tornado, full of energy and his National Recording Company became an entity that housed record labels, a recording studio, publishing companies, and a record promotion center.

Bill rented an old school house in the Brookhaven area of Atlanta around 1960, and built a studio in what was once the lunchroom. The NRC recording engineer was Ivan Miles, an old radio engineer who was the total opposite of Lowery; absolutely nothing impressed or excited Ivan. I can still hear his droll voice coming over the speaker into the recording studio when he flipped on the "record light" saying, "O.K. Let's record this epic." Ivan's "I don't care" attitude was perfect because he did not care what we tried in the studio, so we tried everything. That studio was a great big toy and we played with it night and day.

Because of my musical training, I was always interested in the horn and vocal arrangements of the R&B groups. I liked the simple three chord blues of people like Jimmy Reed with the obligatory guitar or harmonica instrumental in the middle. But it was the "doo-wah" vocals, sax, hand clapping, and more complex arrangements that caught my attention.

We wanted an echo chamber at NRC, but in those days there wasn't a little box you could buy at an electronics store; instead, there were actual chambers that required spending Mucho Dinero and had to be set up in a special room. We found a low-tech solution when we discovered that the old school building where the studios were housed had an unused septic tank buried below it between the building and the parking lot. We had it pumped out and rigged a speaker at one end of the tank and a microphone at the other and ran the sound through it. It worked. From time to time you could hear a distant "bloink" on a track as a drop of water, or something, dripped to the bottom of the tank at an inopportune moment. The day we hooked up the septic tank was the day the "Septic Sounds" of NRC were born.

I had an old upright piano brought in and stuck thumb tacks into all of the felt hammers that struck the strings which made a sharp, bright sound. We kept experimenting with sounds. During a session with Buddy K one day he remembers that I was not getting the sound I wanted from the snare drum so I kept asking the drummer, Tommy South – Joe South's brother – to hit it with different things. He hit it with each end of his regular sticks, with two sticks held together, with brushes, and then the back end of the brushes until I finally said, "What else do you have to hit it with?" Exasperated, Tommy jokingly said, "My shoe." So I said, "Well, hit it with your shoe!" and Voila, there it was, the snare drum sound I was looking for. Ivan just rolled his eyes.

Investors were encouraged to put money into NRC

because of Bill's success with "Be Bop A Lula" and another great Lowery copyright "Young Love." That song stayed at Number One on the National Hit Parade TV Show with Snooky Lanson and Gisele McKenzie for weeks. It was written by Ric Cartey with help, mostly inspirational help I imagine, from his girlfriend Carol Joyner. Carol was a pretty girl and I'm sure she could be downright inspirational. When Ric brought the demo to Lowery, that opening drum lick was made on the tom-toms and sounded like a jungle chant. When Ken Nelson recorded it on Sonny James, the famous Nashville drummer, Buddy Harman, changed the tom-toms to brushes, which really worked for that song. Little things can mean a lot.

"Young Love" was a monster song with hit recordings by Sonny James, movie star Tab Hunter and, a few years later by Leslie Gore. It was a real money maker and financed a lot of young talent, which allowed Lowery to hire more staff.

Felton Jarvis was someone who absolutely loved the music business. He was star struck with Elvis. Eddie Sovine, the second most decorated guy in World War II next to Audie Murphy, wrote a song, "Don't Knock Elvis" when everyone was calling him "Elvis the Pelvis" and putting him down. He played that song for Felton, who said "We have to cut this" so I produced Felton singing "Don't Knock

Elvis" and released it on a label I started, Viva Records. After the release, I received a letter from the famous movie/music man Snuffy Garrett that said, "You can't call your label Viva Records because I already have that name." So I said "O.K." We promoted the record and hoped some big label would pick it up but none did. Felton didn't know one note from another but, with great irony, he ended up producing his hero Elvis!

Felton Jarvis worked for Addressograph Multi-graph, a company that sold printing machines and he talked Lowery into buying a machine to print promotional material for radio, singles sleeves, etc. Bill hired him as a "promotion man" to convince the DJs in the country to play NRC's records. Bill bought some 45 RPM vinyl disk pressing machines from Italy and NRC was doing everything in house. Felton even convinced Bill to hire him to publish a magazine so he was added to the staff.

In those days an independent record company would go fishing with a single record or two on a variety of artists and when a record began to take off at radio, the independent label would sell the record to a major label. Independents were the Research and Development departments for the majors. They spent money to find out if something was a hit in a small region of the country and then, if it looked like it could go national, a major label jumped on it and, through heavy promotion, turned a regional hit into a national smash.

There were lots of independent record producers around as well. One of them was an old country boy named Cleve Warnock. Cleve had a little studio in his Mama's basement and worked with Tommy Roe, a handsome young guy who could write and sing. When Cleve brought Tommy to NRC, Felton was hanging around the studio with a lot of time on his hands because it didn't take long to put out that little magazine every week. He was almost as interested in the studio as I was. Felton took Tommy Roe into the studio and re-recorded his song, "Shelia," with a Buddy Holly style rolling tom-tom rhythm and it caught fire. Felton and Tommy rode that success to amazing heights.

Well, what about Cleve Warnock, you ask? It turned out that Cleve wasn't much of a businessman. For example, he owed NRC several thousand dollars for sessions he couldn't pay for and since NRC was a corporation, the shareholders were hot on Lowery to collect something from this guy. Bill met with Cleve and pleaded with him to make some kind of good faith payment so he could show the Board that the debt was being paid. "Just write me a check that I can show them," Bill pleaded. "I'll even hold it for you for a few days if that will help."

Cleve agreed and promised Bill he'd write a check but

didn't have one with him. Bill countered that "I've got several counter checks in my desk from different Atlanta banks. Which one do you want?" In those days there were only a handful of banks in Atlanta. Cleve replied, "Any one of them. I don't care." Bill was surprised at his response and asked, "You mean you've got money in all the banks in Atlanta?" Whereupon Cleve replied, "No, I don't have money in any bank in Atlanta." Bill then asked, "Well, why would you write me a bad check?" To which Cleve replied, "You're the one who told me to do it!" That pretty much ended the brief record producing career of Cleve Warnock.

CHAPTER 6

In-Laws and Lawyers

Felton was dating a pretty girl named Twinkle Jackson, the secretary of Zenus Sears at the R&B station WAOK. She was from North Carolina and shared a room with her younger sister, Penny. Felton married Twinkle, I married Penny, and we became brothers-in-law as well as friends. This book is about my career and my association with the Nashville music business, not about my family or my personal life. Suffice it to say I fell in love with and married the beautiful Penny Jackson; we have two lovely daughters and four terrific grandchildren. We met way back then and we're still together, over fifty years later.

Felton almost got me killed on more than one occasion. One night he and I went to the Wallahaji Ballroom in the black section of Atlanta to hear Ray Charles. We were the only two white guys who made that decision. We had a ball, but were in the clear minority in a room full of people who were high on Brother Ray's music as well as a little bit of everything else. Felton wasn't satisfied with just being at the concert, he wanted us to go to an All Black after-hours club after the show. We were color blind music lovers but many of the young men who were willing to let well enough alone at the Wallahaji were not so happy to see us at their private club and formulated plans for our removal. The bouncer, a big guy with a deep voice and serious face, came to us and gently said, "Now you boys ain't got no business in here tonight and there's no way I can guarantee your safety so you best be on your way." I didn't wait around for Felton's reply; I was immediately on my way to the car, but Felton got there before I did. We were gone, as Chuck Berry would say, "Like a cool breeze."

My Mama and Daddy were fine with me dabbling in music and recording as long as I didn't neglect the important things in life like a college education. I don't think my Dad ever adjusted to the fact that I was never going to have a real job until he was almost ready to retire.

During the period from 1957 to 1962, I finished high school, spent three years as a music major at Georgia State University in Atlanta, played on and produced numerous sessions for Bill Lowery at NRC Studios as well as in Nashville, and released several records of my own with increasing local and regional success. Still, I did not have a breakout national hit. My record of "Chicky-Chicky-Wah-Wah," recorded in Nashville with the Anita Kerr Singers, came close, but I thought I had found the secret when I wrote and recorded a song about a well-known fictional radio/TV character named "Sergeant Preston of the Yukon." This was in 1959, a year before Dallas Frazier's "Alley-Oop" about an equally famous newspaper comic strip character became a top ten record by three different groups at the same time.

The genesis for "Sergeant Preston" came from my high school days. A friend had an old, beat up green van and a group of us guys would get in and go cruising on Saturday nights. While he was driving, the rest of us would yell, "On King! On you great huskie! (Barking!)" I thought that was damned funny. We'd all seen the TV show, "Sergeant Preston of the Yukon" and so I started with the lines

> In the frozen north of the Yukon
> Lived the King of the Royal Mounted Fuzz
> Sergeant Present was his name,
> And King his dog's name wuz.

On the "Sergeant Preston" record I barked and howled like the Sarge's faithful dog King and his whole canine sled team and made noises like a whip cracking. I talked and sang like the popular jive talking comedians of the day like Brother Dave Gardner. I gave it my best shot, pulled out all the stops and, man, it shot off like a rocket. It was climbing the charts so fast that Lowery was dancing around his office after every phone call that reported our success. A hit! I finally had a *hit*! But then, a few weeks later, Bill called me into his office and, for the first time I could ever remember, he was not enthusiastic. "I've got bad news, lad," he said. "We're going to have to pull the record."

It seems that King Features Syndicate, the people who owned the character "Sergeant Preston," had filed a Cease and Desist order. In other words, we had to exert our best efforts to stop the broadcasting and sale of that record or else they would sue NRC, Bill Lowery Publishing, and Ray Stevens. That would not have meant much to me because I didn't have anything but NRC had shareholders and Bill had other artists whose careers would suffer, so we killed a hit. To this day I don't know why the lawyers didn't react the same way to that threat as they did to songs like "Alley-Oop" and others down through history that featured a cartoon character and capitalize on that song – it was great publicity. But I'm sure that some young lawyer somewhere on the King Features payroll thought this was worthy of their time and effort and completely disregarded the positive impact that song could have on their character. I think Lowery's lawyers were so uninformed that they would have had to call "Information" to get the number for 911. But although it was painful and disappointing, I learned and grew and wrote more songs. I gained experience through the ordeal. Someone said "experience" is what you get when you don't get what you want.

Lowery's lawyers should have been like my friend Bobby Bare. He recorded a song and titled it "God Bless America Again" and it was climbing the charts when a lawyer for Irving Berlin called and told him that he was going to have to take his song off the air. In his slow country way Bobby inquired why he would want to do that and the lawyer reminded him that Mr. Berlin had written the song "God Bless America". Bobby said he didn't get the man's point and the lawyer said the point was that Bobby's song would have no meaning if it weren't for Mr. Berlin's song having been recorded first. Bobby paused for a long time and said "You know, I bet you're not going to like my new Christmas record either." The lawyer curiously asked what the name of that new Bobby Bare Christmas record would be, and Bobby said, "I'm Dreaming of a White Christmas – Again" and hung up before the lawyer could answer.

By 1962, it was crystal clear that NRC was never going to be RCA and that when it came to being a recording center, Atlanta was never going to be Nashville. Nashville was the epicenter of opportunity for singers and songwriters of Country, Pop and Rock. Shelby Singleton, a friend of Bill's from Shreveport, Louisiana, who started as a local promotion man for Mercury Records in Louisiana after he finished his tour of duty with the Marines, became the key connection that brought me to Nashville for good.

CHAPTER 7

Good-Bye Atlanta, Hello Nashville

I first met Shelby Singleton at a little show called The Georgia Jubilee, which was produced every Saturday by a radio station in East Point, Georgia. There was a matinee, and evening show, and I was an opening act. Everybody in Lowery's stable of singers took turns playing that show and, after the opening slot, they'd bring in The Big Act, the Headliner. One week they brought in The Big Bopper – J.P. Richardson – who had a new record that was at the top of the charts, "Chantilly Lace." Shelby was the promotion guy for Mercury and he watched me play and open the show, and then we met backstage.

Sometime after our meeting he was promoted to head of A&R for the Nashville office and moved from Shreveport to Nashville. Shelby didn't know one note from another, so he brought guitar player Jerry Kennedy with him because Jerry is a great musician and could help Shelby make records. With Shelby's ear and Jerry's musicianship, they made a great combination and they signed a bunch of acts. He needed help with all those acts so he called his old friend Bill Lowery. It didn't have to be a long distance call. The Mercury Records office was in the Cumberland Lodge Building on Seventh Avenue in Nashville, and so were the offices for the Wilburn Brothers, Tree Music, and Lowery Music's Nashville office.

Shelby and Jerry were new to Nashville, but they were beginning to make some noise and needed extra help. Specifically, Shelby needed someone to sort through and listen to all the songs submitted for artists on the Mercury label and find suitable material for them to record. After that person found songs for an artist, he needed to rehearse the artist prior to the recording session. Sounded like something I could do so I answered the call.

At that time I was also signed to Mercury as a recording artist, and had recorded "Jeremiah Peabody's Poly Unsaturated Quick Dissolving Fast Acting Pleasant Tasting Green and Purple Pills," which was my first national chart record after "Sergeant Preston of the Yukon." Shelby had noticed.

Bill Lowery told me that Shelby had called about me and asked, "Do you want to go to Nashville?" I said "I don't know." I then called Shelby and asked, "What do you pay?" When Shelby told me that I would make the magnificent sum of $50 a week, my spirits were dashed. "I can't live off $50 a week," I told him. "I have a wife and new baby and

I can't afford to move across town, much less 250 miles for that amount. At least in Atlanta I got a free Sunday dinner with my family from time to time." Shelby explained that he would hire me for every Mercury session in some capacity so that I would make the session pay as well as my salary. Shelby knew that I had done a number of sessions in Atlanta as well as in Nashville. The potential pay from two or three sessions a day for two or three days every week was plenty to sweeten the deal, so I jumped at the opportunity and moved from Atlanta to Nashville on January 2, 1962.

Shelby was true to his word; I worked lots of sessions. On January 20, I was booked for three sessions one day, including one I had booked for myself. This was my first session since moving to Nashville and becoming part of the Nashville musical community. In those days, you generally recorded four songs in three hours and I was short one song. So the night before that session, I created a character of my own and wrote a song about him. His name was "Ahab the Arab the Sheik of the Burning Sand." I remembered the formula that had worked on "Sergeant Preston" so, instead of a barking dog I had a braying camel and I threw in references to the "Grand Ole Opry," current songs like "The Twist" and "Does Your Chewing Gum Lose Its Flavor on the Bedpost Overnight."

The idea came from a book I read as a kid, *Tales of the Arabian Nights*. My mom was big on giving me books and she gave me that one as well as books on Robin Hood, *The Illiad* and *The Odyssey*. When I read *Arabian Nights,* I thought that Ali Baba and the Forty Thieves, "open ses- ame" and those things were really neat. So I figured, hey, I'll just write me a song about an Arab. I was living in a little apartment in Madison, a Nashville suburb, on Ardee Avenue, off Gallatin Road. It was an upstairs apartment with one bedroom, a kitchen, living room, and bathroom. That was my first home in Nashville. I had a wife and baby girl, Timi Lynn, and she was sleeping in a dresser drawer. It was the bottom drawer.

It was late at night when I went into the kitchen, sat down and started that song. I think what attracted me to the idea was that I could make weird noises. I didn't know what a camel sounded like so I made up a sound that turned out to be right. It took me an hour or less to write that song and when I finished it I thought, "That's a hit!"

Shelby Singleton produced that session in the Quonset Hut, where we did most of our recording. The session was at ten o'clock that morning and I came in a little before then, wrote out a chord chart with numbers – the Nashville number system – gave a copy to each of the musicians, sat down at the piano and said, "This is the way it goes." Jerry

Kennedy played guitar on that session, Buddy Harman was on drums, and I sang as I played the piano.

I pulled out all the stops on that recording. It happened fast – there weren't any do-overs or overdubs. Just cut it straight through.

That was not a usual day of Nashville sessions because something happened that day that I don't believe ever happened before or since. My session was from ten to one. The two o'clock session was for Leroy Van Dyke, who recorded "Walk on By," a song published by Bill Lowery. I was also on the six o'clock session that evening when Joe Dowell recorded "Wooden Heart." I played organ on that session. All three of those songs were big hits on the charts. That was magic and not a bad day's work for a young guy who had just moved to Nashville. As a matter of fact, it was downright encouraging when my risky move was rewarded with my first bona fide hit.

I did a lot of session work. Word got around fast and the word was that I was quick to learn, had good ideas to contribute to the session, was always available and I could play piano, double on vocals, and play just about anything else a producer discovered he needed during a session. Pig Robbins, a great session piano player, said the most important thing he ever learned was "when not to play," and I learned that too. It helped to be hungry, agreeable and connected. People were throwing work my way all the time.

Bill Lowery always used me whenever he came to town with his acts from Atlanta to record. Chet Atkins knew me before I got to town and often hired me. When Felton Jarvis, my brother-in-law, came to work at RCA as an A&R man for Chet, the network grew. In addition to all the session work and song searches for other acts, I still had my own recording career and a new contract with Mercury just to keep it all in the family.

CHAPTER 8

Country Humor

"Ahab the Arab" was a big hit and earned me the reputation as a comedy song artist and as a "funny man" from the very start. While the song was a hit on Pop, Country, and some R&B Stations, the humor is pure Country and a product of my raising and experience.

People think I'm funny, and I have seen articles written about me that say I "think" funny. Well that might be true because I do spend a lot of time thinking about things that other people might not. Like, have you ever wondered about cured ham? I mean what did it have . . . and is it alright to eat it now, after having been so sick and all?

That's the kind of humor I grew up around and the kind of humor that is in all my jokes and songs. I'm like a blue serge suit going through life picking up pieces of humorous lint and using them in my routines and music. We are all products of our environments and none of us get much above our raising, as they say back home.

If I'm funny at all, it is because I am funny to a specific group of people – people like me. You have to know your audience – and I am a really good example of my audience. If I think it is funny, then I probably know several million other people who will think it's funny, too. I doubt that the question, "Have you heard Ray Stevens' latest humor?," is ever uttered at a New York After-Theatre dinner or on the Washington D.C. cocktail circuit. But it plays real well around the cracker barrel and there are a lot more cracker barrels in America and Australia, Canada and England than one might think.

One night on the Johnny Carson Show, the comedian David Brenner mentioned the name of another comic and commented how famous he was. Johnny said, "Hold it. Famous? I've never heard of him. How 'famous' can he be?" Brenner launched into a tutorial that has stuck with me ever since. He explained that there were about 250 million people in the U.S.A. at that time and that if a person had 2.5 million people who were wild about them, went to all their concerts and bought their records or books or whatever, then they would be wealthy and famous while 99% of the population might not even know about them at all. It's true. Being famous or popular or successful is a relative thing. I'm sure there are Hip Hop millionaires or famous cat jugglers or Opera Divas who are wildly popular that I have never heard of in my sheltered life.

Southern humor, Country humor, has its audience and

it's a big one. At least big enough for me, because I have sold over 25 million recordings, 6 million Videos and DVDs and had over 60 million unique views on YouTube Videos while most people in the world have never even heard of me. Those numbers may be low to some folks, but they have helped me make a good living.

Country humor is all about country people. It is self-deprecating, focused on ourselves. The cartoon character Pogo famously said, "We have spied the enemy and they is us." Well southern people have seen who is funny, and it is us and our relatives. My friend and great songwriter, Norro Wilson, is from Scottsville, Kentucky, about an hour up the road from Nashville and he always talks about his Uncle Coy. Coy was famous in Scottsville for telling tall tales. No one could lie like Coy. Country folks are funny that way, we admire honesty but people get applauded for being such a big liar too, and southern kids argue about whose Dad can deliver the most painful whuppin.'

One day Norro said he and his Mom and Dad were sitting on their front porch just rocking in their rocking chairs and sipping on sweet tea on a hot summer afternoon, when they saw Uncle Coy walking up the dirt road in front of their house in an unusual hurry with a look of stern determination on his face. Norro's Daddy laughed and yelled, "Hey there Coy. What you up to? Why don't you come over here and tell us a lie and make us believe it?" Norro said Coy didn't even turn his head their way and as he kept his pace he yelled out, "I ain't got time to mess with you. I'm on my way to Delbert and Imogene's. Delbert just fell off his mowing machine dead!" Well they jumped up and said, "Lord have mercy! Poor Delbert! Poor Imogene! We need to fix some dinner and take it to the house. Oh Lord, poor Imogene!"

Norro said about an hour later, he and his Mom and Dad pulled up in Delbert and Imogene's yard all bathed and dressed like they were going to church with a fine country dinner of chicken and biscuits in a basket only to see Delbert on his mowing machine cutting hay in the side pasture and Coy sitting on the front porch sipping tea with Imogene and smiling. He had told them a lie and made them believe it just like they'd asked.

Norro said that Coy lied so much that he had to get someone else to call his dog for him.

Jerry Clower was a master Southern storyteller and his characters were always his boyhood friends like Marcel Ledbetter, but one of my favorite stories he told is an excellent example of southern humor. Jerry said that he and his wife, Homerlene, had moved into a nice new subdivision and became friends with the folks next door with whom they would sit on their deck in the backyard and enjoy coffee and conversation. The neighbor lady raised big, beautiful rabbits and when they went away for a long weekend they arranged for someone to feed and water them while they were gone. Well, the Clower's owned a big German Shepherd and as they were sitting on their deck having coffee the day after their neighbors left for vacation, they saw their dog with one of the prized rabbits in its mouth, all covered with mud and blood and violently shaking it back and forth. They ran out and got the rabbit away from the dog, but it was dead as a hammer, limp as a noodle. They didn't know what to do, but Homerlene took that dead, muddy rabbit inside and washed it off, gave it a shampoo and dried it with a hairdryer and brushed its fur neat as could be and took it over and put it back in its cage. When their friends came home they said nothing. The next day the four of them were having coffee in the backyard when the neighbor said, "You know, the strangest thing happened." "Really?" Jerry and Homerlene replied, acting ignorant. The neighbor said, "The night before we left, one of our rabbits died and we buried it in the backyard, but when we came home yesterday it was back in its cage looking like it had just come back from the beauty parlor!"

I had the opportunity to work with Jerry a couple of times. I recorded a song titled "Southern Air" written by Brent Holmes and Stuart Dill and was joined by Jerry, whose voice was that of a hillbilly airline pilot, and Minnie Perl, who was the stewardess. Jerry was also in my music video movie *Get Serious*.

I love Country Humor. I grew up with it and have been laughing at country people and their stories all my life. It's clean and wholesome and draws on a shared life experience. It's like the Yiddish Humor of the Catskills, or Irish Pub humor. It's cultural and thankfully there are millions of people who share that culture with me and enjoy it too. Most of my comedy songs are full of it. I don't think "I think funny" like that reporter said; I think I think "Country." My life experience, full of funny stories and funny ways of saying things, is what has influenced my writing and performing. Even though I was initially considered a Pop singer when I came to Nashville, I shared many life experiences with the Country music singers and musicians here, and that made me feel right at home.

CHAPTER 9

Rock 'N' Roll Record Promotion

The record business was pretty simple in the early days of my career. Singers recorded songs, radio stations played them, people listened, and the recording artists became popular. Disc jockeys became popular, too, because listeners connected with their favorite local DJs, who played records and did their jive talk. It was entertainment. Radio stations played a variety of music: slow, fast, vocals, instrumentals, and novelty songs. In addition to presenting listeners with an entertaining program, the DJs were also local businessmen and they rented movie theaters for a Saturday afternoon and put on a show. The record promotion men got the DJs to play their artist's records and made the artist available to perform on the show for a piece of the gate. Or, more often than not – FREE. Everybody was happy.

A record promotion man travelled with an artist to a radio station for interviews and to their shows at local clubs or high school gyms. On most of those shows, a band was there who learned the song from the record and replicated the rhythm track in the right key. The artist stood up and did their song.

I started going out to promote my current release when I had "Jeremiah Peabody's Poly Unsaturated Quick Dissolving Fast Acting Pleasant Tasting Green and Purple Pills." That record made it to number 35 on the Hot 100 – that's the pop chart – in *Billboard*. It was a minor sensation nationally, but a much bigger deal in the Southeast so that's where I worked. This was before "Ahab the Arab." The money I made was not so much, but it was a big deal to do promotion for the record company. The promotion man took me from one radio station interview to the next and drummed up sales for my record. There were a lot of afternoon TV dance party shows too, local replications of the big "American Bandstand" show in Philadelphia hosted by Dick Clark. At these, I would lip-sync my latest record and advertise my local appearances.

All of that activity is pretty forgettable except for a couple of experiences. Once, Paul Cochran, a show promoter from Clearwater, Florida, and I were doing all of the above across the Sunshine State. Paul worked for the city of Clearwater and booked inexpensive acts for local entertainment. He was responsible for the receipts from the shows and record sales at the venue. He had a simple accounting system: He kept the receipts from each show in a separate paper sack in his trunk. Since this was strictly a cash business, there were a number of brown paper sacks filled with mostly ones and five dollar bills after we'd been on the road for a week or so.

We were on the Sunshine Parkway on a bridge across Tampa Bay. We had been to Clearwater, Tampa, and St. Petersburg, and were driving toward Bradenton and then on to the East Coast. I was sitting in the passenger seat, pretty bored, so I started checking out Paul's new Oldsmobile. I complimented him on the front seat, the back seat, the dashboard, and opened the glove compartment, where I saw a button. As I pushed that button I asked, "What is this?" Paul screamed, "Don't push that!" It was too late. That button opened the trunk, which flew up while we were going 70 miles an hour and ones and fives flew out of that trunk in a big cloud and rained down all over the highway.

Paul hit the brakes, swerved to the shoulder of the road and we jumped out and picked up money as we dodged the oncoming traffic until we couldn't find any more. After we'd picked up all the money we could find, we faced the problem of which sacks did each of the bills come from? Almost everything that Paul Cochran said to me during the next hour is unprintable.

I have no idea how he handled the accounting when we got back, but I made sure that I got me one of those cars with a button that opened the trunk as soon as I could.

I bought my first Cadillac with a button in the glove box with money from my first hit record. Wesley Rose told me that it was a really dumb thing to do because I might not ever have another hit or another Cadillac. Thank goodness he was wrong.

There were all of those individual appearances where I lip-synced my hit or played with a pick-up house band, and then there were the package tours. The General Artists Corporation, known as GAC, was one of the big agencies that put together Rock'n'Roll bus tours. In 1961, I was booked on a big GAC tour and we left New York City with a tour manager named Jesse Strumm and stayed out for thirty days. It almost killed me. For that whole tour I made $2,500, and I saved $2,300 of it. In those days you could live on the road pretty cheaply; we stayed in cheap hotels and ate horribly. I remember one night I called the front desk of an especially cheap hotel and the rude night clerk growled, "What's eating you?" and I told him, "That's what I'd like to know!"

I was on that tour with Tony Orlando, back before there was an "and Dawn." He'd had a minor hit and was part of the group that included all those great writers at the Brill

Building in New York – like Neil Sedaka, Barry Mann, Cynthia Weil, Gerry Goffin and Carole King, who wrote hits like "Be My Baby," "Will You Still Love Me Tomorrow," "Up On The Roof," "You've Lost That Lovin' Feeling" and "The Loco-Motion."

Bobby Vinton's band played for all of us. Bobby had a record out, but this was before "Blue Velvet" and all those other great hits he had. The girl singer was Janie Grant, who was almost a one hit wonder. Her biggest hit was "Triangle," which got to number 29 on the pop charts. The show was rounded out by Ral Donner who sang like Elvis, but wasn't. I don't know what ever happened to Janie or Ral.

Dick Clark organized tours – Dick Clark's American Bandstand Review – and on one of those tours was Paul and Paula, who had a big hit with "Hey, Paula." That record had come out on La Cam, a small label headed by Major Bill Smith in Fort Worth, Texas, and Shelby Singleton heard it, bought the rights, and released it on a label under the Mercury umbrella. Shelby had great ears; that record was number one for three weeks straight in 1963.

The original record was released with "Jill and Ray" listed as the artists, because the singers were Jill Jackson and Ray Hildebrand. Shelby decided to release it under the names "Paul and Paula" because it was a love song where the two singers pledged eternal love. Those who heard the record logically assumed that Paul and Paula were sweethearts, but that was not the case.

Ray Hildebrand was seriously involved with a young lady named Judy back in Texas, who later became his wife, and the make-believe romance contrived by the record company was getting in the way of his real life romance. This put a great deal of pressure on Ray to fly to the arms of his true love, so he left the tour before it was over. This was a brave, bold move but it effectively ended his Rock'n'Roll career, as well as the career of Paul and Paula, but a man's gotta do what a man's gotta do.

Jill remained with the tour for the rest of the run and continued singing that song to audiences with the part of Paul sung by none other than Dick Clark! As they say in the biz, the show must go on. Ray Hildebrand went on to record and release the very first ever Contemporary Christian Album for Word Records that included a big hit, "Say I Do."

I've heard stories about payola in those days, and I have no reason to doubt those stories. Then again, there is always some sort of quid pro quo in any business. I showed up and performed on someone's live show or made an appearance on a television show with no pay, in exchange for airplay of my records, so I guess that's a form of payola.

It's the same thing when a salesman takes a client to lunch or for a round of golf at the country club. In the movies *Ray* and *Cadillac Records,* label executives like Jerry Wexler at Atlantic Records and Leonard Chess at Chess Records – as well as many others – simply gave disc jockeys money to play their records in key markets. At least that's the way it's portrayed in the movies.

I do know that Colonel Tom Parker had Otis Blackwell give up part of his songwriting royalties to Elvis for "All Shook Up" and "Don't Be Cruel."

During the 1980s, when payola had supposedly been cleaned up and didn't exist anymore, I was at a cocktail party celebrating the success of one of my albums that had two big hit singles released from it. The head of the record company apologized because that album had not gone to the top of the charts. "Don't worry," he said. "Your next album will go Number One." Amazingly, it did hit Number One on the charts even though it contained no hit singles. How 'bout them apples?

CHAPTER 10

Studio Work

In the northwest corner of Alabama is the tri-cities area of Muscle Shoals, Florence, and Tuscumbia; the Muscle Shoals-Florence area is known as "The Shoals." It's about an hour and a half drive from Nashville to get there. In Muscle Shoals, Rick Hall established Fame Recording Studio with Billy Sherrill. Billy sold his share of the studio and moved to Nashville, where he became a legendary producer of country acts. Billy produced hits on Tammy Wynette, George Jones, as well as George and Tammy, Tanya Tucker, and David Houston.

Rick Hall was another person who knew Bill Lowery, because Bill often took his acts to Rick's Fame Studios to record as well as to Nashville. After I moved to Nashville, I often traveled to Muscle Shoals to work as a musician on his sessions and as an arranger and producer. That's how I first met Jerry Carrigan, David Briggs, and Norbert Putnam, the great pickers who made up the original Muscle Shoals rhythm section. There was something about Muscle Shoals that created that funky swamp music sound those guys got down there. Felton Jarvis recorded Tommy Roe's "Everybody," which was the follow up hit to "Sheila," and Bill Lowery recorded "What Kind of Fool" by The Tams, a Rhythm and Blues group from Atlanta, there.

Those sessions began a fantastic run of hits for five or six years, then many of those Muscle Shoals musicians rode their reputations up to Nashville, where recording sessions were more frequent, and they became first-call musicians and creative producers here. However, the legacy of that studio and the musicians who remained in Alabama continued to expand the Muscle Shoals sound throughout the music world.

Mac Davis, who lived in Atlanta for a while and worked for Lowery in the early days, took a job as a West Coast record promotion man for the rhythm and blues label, VeeJay. Mac also signed with VeeJay as an artist. That VeeJay connection came from Lowery through his friend Steve Clark, another promotion man. Mac recorded several hit singles and gold albums, then had a popular TV show and movie career. Whenever it came time to record, Mac Davis traveled all of the way from Los Angeles to Muscle Shoals to work with the Fame Gang. Over the years, artists such as Tom Jones, Paul Simon, Aretha Franklin, Little Richard, Bob Segar, The Rolling Stones, and many others did the same thing. The Stones cut "Brown Sugar" and "Wild Horses," Aretha cut "I Never Loved a Man (The Way

I Love You)," and Paul Simon cut "Loves Me Like a Rock" in Muscle Shoals.

The years I spent working as a session musician was a great, fun time in my life. There's nothing like the creative process when you are in a studio with a group of talented, creative individuals. On a session, all the musicians stand around and listen to a demo tape, or the artist plays a new song live on piano or guitar, and then the creative juices begin to flow from every part of the room. Sometimes it's almost electric. Everyone has a pencil and piece of paper and, as the song or tape is played, each musician marks the bars and chord changes. Nashville studio musicians developed the Number System by assigning a number from one to seven instead of chords. That means the chord sheet can be transposed into any key. Minor chords are notated by a minus sign, augmented chords by a plus sign, and seventh chords by the number 7. Then there is a brief discussion about notations, pushes or breaks. The numbers indicate the song's chord pattern so the key doesn't matter.

For example, let's say a song is in the key of "C." C is number 1, F is 4 and G is 5. If there is an A minor that would be 6-. This might mean the song is written as:

1 4 5 5

6- 5 1 1

Translated, this means the song starts in C for one measure, goes to F for a measure, then to G for two measures, then to A minor for a measure, then to G and then two measures back on C.

If the singer decides that key is too low and wants to raise it to D, the numbers remain the same because the musicians know how each number relates to the chord in a song. So, in the new key, the chords are D to G then to A, B minor and A again before it goes back to D.

The musicians play the song through once and discuss ideas. Someone standing in the control room can hear them "noodling" on their instruments as they work up an intro, or the lead instrumental on a break as players offer options and licks for the producer to choose from. The producer's role is to listen and decide which ideas to incorporate. The producer may say "Hey, I like that – give me some more of it" or "Yeah, that's good but try to lay back a little and let me hear it on the bridge." Most producers give the pickers an idea of what they have in mind and then the musicians give him their interpretations and the producer pulls it together. Many producers do little more than let the guys do their thing during the session and then apply their part during the mixing process while other producers have a definite idea of what they want played.

I learned a lot during those days and played on more

sessions than I can recall, but there were a few sessions that stand out. I was booked on an Elvis session once and usually played piano and organ, but the producer wanted a double Spanish trumpet sound on one of the tracks. I don't remember the song, but I remember the producer was going to call a trumpet player when Charlie McCoy, the famous harmonica player, and I spoke up and said we each had a trumpet in our car. We ran out, got them, and laid down those parts. I also played trumpet on the Elvis recording of "Fools Fall in Love" that was originally recorded by Clyde McPhatter and the Drifters.

On another session, Chet was recording Waylon Jennings and felt the title line of the song, "You've Got the Only Daddy That'll Walk the Line" needed a high harmony part so he called me in. I had to stand on my tippy toes to do that high harmony with Waylon, but that's me on that famous hit record.

I traveled to a studio in Cincinnati, Ohio, to record Jimmie Skinner, the famous bluegrass singer and when a young girl from East Tennessee first came to town to record for Monument Records, I was given the task of finding material for her, rehearsing her, and producing her first record. That was Dolly Parton. The session I produced with her wasn't a hit, but I understand she did well after that.

In 1965, I left Mercury and accepted a position with Monument Records as I tried to broaden my career with a little more serious direction. I had some success with *Even Stevens*, an album I released, and a single, "Unwind."

I joined Monument to record for Fred Foster, who owned the label. Monument was named for the Washington Monument in our nation's capital, where Fred was from. He had moved his operation from Washington to Hendersonville, about twenty miles north of Nashville, so every day I made a 45 minute drive up US 31 to work in the record company with Fred as A&R for new artists like Dolly Parton and others, as well as work on my own recording career.

Fred Foster was born in Rutherford County, North Carolina and, at a young age, his father died so he supported his mother. He left home when he was seventeen and moved to Washington, D.C., where he worked for ABC Paramount and Mercury Records. Soon, young Fred wanted his own record company so, with partial funding from Buddy Deane, a local disc jockey, he started Monument Records in 1957. The first record Monument released was "Gotta Travel On" by Billy Grammer, which was a huge success. From that point on, Fred seemed to have a knack for picking winners.

When I joined Monument, other acts on the label included

Roy Orbison and the great saxophone player Boots Randolph. Boots and I played on a lot of sessions together. Through the years, other artists on Monument included Willie Nelson, Kris Kristofferson, Tommy Roe, Tony Joe White, Connie Smith, and Larry Gatlin and his younger brothers, Steve and Rudy. Everybody knew the Gatlins were going to be stars, but it took a while for them to click. Fred had a great roster and made some great records.

About the time I came to Monument, Fred hired Mike Shepherd, a West Coast promotion man, who had been working for Reprise, the label owned by Frank Sinatra. Mike's real name is Myron Schector and he is a Russian Jew from the Bronx. Although Mike left New York in 1958, his accent sounds like he just moved south yesterday. He and I have a long history that started in Hendersonville, where he still lives, and has lasted decades, a million miles and as many laughs, and several record companies. I worked with Mike every day during the last few years until he recently retired to a life of Golf and Tennis.

My experience as a Nashville session player has paid great dividends over the years because when I make records these days I am able to work alone with just an engineer and I lay down all the drum and bass, piano tracks and vocals. Like I told someone the other day, I may not be the best drummer, bass man, background singer or piano man in town but I am the best in my price range. I'm proud to be known as a Nashville Cat. That's the Country Music Hall of Fame title for a Nashville session player.

CHAPTER 11

Hello, It's Hollywood!

During my time at Monument, my career began to blossom and my session work became less and less as I found national and international success as an artist, but I established important relationships that shaped my career for years to come.

I met Bill Justis during the time I was doing sessions. Bill started his career in Memphis working at Sun Records for Sam Phillips. At Sun, he produced and arranged sessions for the Sun acts and had a Rock n'Roll instrumental hit of his own with his saxophone classic "Raunchy," which is now in the Grammy Hall of Fame.

Justis was a "cat." He was a jive talking sax man who knew how to write horn and string charts and taught me more in a day or two than I learned during all my years as a Music Major at Georgia State. He worked at Mercury and Monument, and seemed to be a constant presence in those early days. Bill Lowery also used him on sessions at NRC in Atlanta.

When Justis produced a session, he always livened it

up with the charts he handed musicians. If the song to be recorded was "Cry Me a River," he might pass out a chart to the guitar player that said "Fry Me a Liver," and the one to the bass player might say "Buy Me A Fliver." It was a unique ice breaker and calling card to loosen up a bunch of young musicians who rarely saw a chart during a recording session. Although the studio musicians generally used the casual short hand number system and worked up an arrangement in the studio, here was a guy who knew exactly what he wanted you to play.

We were in the coffee shop of the Continental Hotel in Los Angeles one day when Justis said to me, "I got a title for you man. 'Gitar-Zan.' Get it? 'Gitar-Zan!'" And then he chuckled.

I came back to Nashville and was set to record, but needed a song. I had just bought a rhyming dictionary – *The Clement C. Wood Rhyming Dictionary* – with a green cover. I didn't know there was such a thing as a rhyming dictionary before then. "Gitarzan" was the first song I wrote using it. I'd write a line and then put as many rhymes in it as I could. I didn't bother with meter while I wrote, then I'd change chords and come up with another line and continue the story, change chords again, write another line and put in as many rhymes as I could. When I finished I thought, "Boy, this is pretty good!" Notice how

I often think that about songs I've written?

It was a song that was fun to produce and record. I did it at Bradley's Barn studio in Mount Juliet, Tennessee, just outside Nashville near Old Hickory Lake. When "Gitarzan" was finished, I was thrilled with it and Mike Shepherd thought it was a monster. Fred Foster didn't care for it at all, and did not want to release it. Mike and I assured Fred that this was a smash and leaned on him until he finally agreed to release "Gitarzan" on Monument. To sweeten the deal, I promised Fred that if it was not a hit, he could produce all my sessions from that time on.

Fred never got the chance to produce me because "Gitarzan" was a wildfire of a hit. It was played everywhere, and I mean everywhere. Pop, Country, R&B, U.S.A., U.K. everywhere. Everywhere I went I'd hear "Shut up baby, I'm tryin' to sing." Bill Justis was right, "Gitarzan" was a great title. That record reached number eight on *Billboard's* Hot 100 here in the U.S.A. and then, Hollywood called.

The Hollywood phone call came from Burt Bacharach and Hal David, who flew me to Los Angeles to play a song they had written for a movie. Bacharach and David were legendary songwriters. The string of hits they wrote would fill a book, so I'll just name a few: "Blue on Blue" by Bobby Vinton, "Magic Moments" by Perry Como, "Wishin' and

Hopin'" by Dusty Springfield, "What the World Needs Now" by Jackie DeShannon, a Marty Robbins hit, "The Story of My Life," and a long string of hits for Dionne Warwick that includes "Don't Make Me Over," "Walk on By," "Anyone Who Had a Heart" and "Message to Michael." They had a track record with movies, too. They wrote "What's It All About, Alfie" and "The Man Who Shot Liberty Valance." They hit on Broadway with the score to *Promises Promises*.

I flew to L.A., rented a car and drove to Burt's house in the Hollywood Hills where he played the song for me that he wanted me to sing. The movie the song was to appear in was *Butch Cassidy and the Sundance Kid*, which starred Paul Newman and Robert Redford, and the song was "Raindrops Keep Fallin' On My Head." They wanted me to record it and release it as part of the promotion for the movie, so they had a strict timetable that was tied to a world-wide release and coordinated advertising campaign. Things had to move quickly; there was no wiggle room.

I loved the song but had a problem. A few weeks before I had gone to Los Angeles, Nashville publisher Bob Beckham brought three songs to me. Bob was the head of Combine Publishing, which was the publishing arm of Fred Foster's Monument Records. He was a good friend who had worked for Bill Lowery, which is where I first met him.

The songs were written by a new songwriter who was

signed to his company and was writing some killer material. He was a Rhodes Scholar, ex-Army serviceman named Kris Kristofferson, and on that tape were "Me and Bobby McGee," "Help Me Make It Through the Night" and "Sunday Morning Comin' Down." Bob told me to "pick one" and I selected "Sunday Morning Comin' Down" and decided that would be my next single release. For weeks I worked on it in the studio. I thought this would be my masterpiece and, major motion picture release or not, I was not about to delay what I thought was an absolute home run, hands down, number one smash just to sing a song – which I thought was a great song – for a cowboy picture. And so I passed and did not record "Raindrops Keep Fallin' On My Head."

Not long ago, I told that story to B.J. Thomas – whose version of "Raindrops Keep Fallin' On My Head" was number one on the pop chart for four consecutive weeks in 1970 – while we rode together in a van going to a taping for a PBS Television Special in St. Louis. He stood up, leaned over two rows of seats, and said "Thank You!" That was B.J.'s song. What a singer he is. I have never heard anyone who is a more natural born singer in my life. Somehow, all things really do work together for good.

And how, you might ask, did Ray Stevens' epic recording of "Sunday Morning Comin' Down" do? Well, I must admit that it was a bomb at radio, but it is still one of my personal favorites of all the records I've done. I suppose that people could not imagine me singing about waking up stoned on a Sunday morning. Come to think of it, the people were right, because I never ever woke up in that condition.

"Sunday Morning Comin' Down" didn't hurt my career because it pretty much went unnoticed. Then I got another call from Hollywood. Roger Miller's manager, Don Williams, was with Bernard, Williams, and Price, the Los Angeles group who managed Bob Newhart and Mary Tyler Moore, among others. Don was Andy Williams' brother and Roger told him that he should represent me, too. Roger told Don that I was an up and coming unique Nashville talent who had no management and needed good representation – and that's how I met my good friend Donald J. Williams.

During the late 1940s and early 1950s, The Williams Brothers were a hot nightclub act who headlined shows all over the country and appeared in movies and on television with Kay Thompson. The Williams Brothers broke up as an act, but Andy, the youngest brother, continued a show business career in New York. Andy Williams recorded for Archie Blyer on his Cadence label, and was a regular on "The Tonight Show Starring Steve

Allen" along with the singing duo of Steve Lawrence and Edye Gorme.

In 1962, Andy Williams became the host of a popular TV variety show on NBC that ran for ten years. Andy's show was a very musical, yet comedic show and a perfect place for me and my material. Nothing builds celebrity like television, and I was about to do more and more of it.

Don lived in Hollywood and had been a booking agent for Las Vegas night clubs. He looked more like Andy Williams than Andy himself to some people, and was the most affable and nicest guy you ever met. Don had been in show business in Hollywood, on the road on the night club circuit, and had done movies. He was old school show biz and one classy guy. We hit it off right away. He had a zany sense of humor and was a perfect representative for the likes of Roger Miller and Ray Stevens.

Don took charge of my career, arranged for me to connect with a West Coast accounting firm, introduced me to Andy's Hollywood tailor, signed me up with the prestigious William Morris Agency, and booked me on some guest appearances on the highly-rated "Andy Williams Show" on NBC. When my contract with Monument and Fred Foster was up, both Mike Shepherd and I joined Andy Williams' record company, Barnaby, which established offices in Nashville on Music Row. Mike then made the daily drive from Hendersonville into Nashville, instead of me driving 45 minutes the other way and my Barnaby years commenced.

CHAPTER 12

Fun Backstage

One of the perks of being in Show Business and having some success is that you get to meet and hang out with people you admire and probably wouldn't have a chance to meet otherwise. I'm a fan, just like most people, and while it's hard for me to grasp the idea that people would actually want my autograph or want to have their picture taken with me, I totally get it when it comes to artists and entertainers that I admire.

Bobby Goldsboro is a fun guy to hang with. When he was recording his string of hits here in Nashville, I got called to sing high harmony with him on several sessions. Bobby sings pretty high already and I had to stand on a stool to reach some of those notes. Our paths have crossed on the road numerous times over the years, and it is fun to meet up with Bobby and his wife, Diane, for dinner after a show. His road manager, Jim Stephany, worked for me for a number of years during a period when Bobby was working on TV projects that kept him at home.

At that taping of a fund raising show for National Public

Television in St. Louis I mentioned earlier that included B.J. Thomas, there was also Billy Joe Royal, Goldie and me among others, like Marvin Hamlisch, Peaches and Herb, but we were the four (me, Goldsboro, B.J. and Billy Joe) that had a history together and so we really enjoyed renewing old friendships during the long hours of us doing nothing. TV production entails a lot of "Hurry up and wait." Billy Joe Royal has a vocal routine he goes through to loosen up his vocal chords before he goes out on stage and sometimes it requires a lot of "clearing the throat" noises. Sometimes he has more difficulty clearing his throat than others and it can go on and on and on. One night, Billy Joe was going through a rather protracted session of throat clearing gymnastics in the next room. We were separated by only a partial wall. As the noises continued, Bobby got up and walked around the wall and said to Billy Joe, "Billy, if you ever get that thing up I want to see it!" We all fell down laughing.

Bobby is a talented guy. He produced his own Kids Show for PBS titled "Swamp Critters" where he and Diane perform most of the "critters" tunes in full raccoon and possum costumes, etc. to tracks of songs that Bobby wrote and produced with him playing all of the instruments and doing all of the voices. He did a similar thing when he produced the sound tracks each week for Burt Reynolds "Evening

Shade" weekly network TV program. He had a TV show of his own back in the 60s and 70s for three or four years. One day not long ago, Bobby told me that he got a call from Willie Nelson who had bought all of his old shows in a package deal he made whereby Willie had acquired lots of TV programming for a Cowboy Channel he was trying to put together. Willie told Bobby he had the shows and really didn't need them for his venture. When Bobby asked Willie what he wanted for them, how much could he buy them from Willie for, he was shocked when Willie said he wanted to give them to Bobby, no charge. What a guy!

Bobby is from Dothan in South Alabama, and is a good guitar player and a heck of a songwriter. When he went off to college, he formed a band and they were popular on campus. They had such a reputation that a guy approached them one day and asked if they would like to be the road band for an entertainer that was looking for a good band to travel with him. When Bobby heard that the entertainer was Roy Orbison, he jumped at the chance and jumped right out of college and into the record business. It wasn't long before he had a recording contract of his own. You never know what door is going to open for you on the road to following your dream.

Living in Nashville, I get called on to do appearances at the Grand Ole Opry House for either the long running week-end radio and sometimes TV show, but also many Specials and Awards Shows are taped there. It's an opportunity for many in the business to be together for a day or two and sit around for hours waiting your turn to go on for five minutes. You can hear some great picking and great behind-the-scenes stories at those events.

Grandpa Jones was a character. Actually he was a character created by a teenager named Louis Marshall Jones during his High School years in Akron, Ohio. I guess Grandpa spent the next sixty odd years growing into the part. The stories about him would fill several books but I can only report a couple of them here. I heard them straight from Grandpa when backstage at the Opry or on the set of "Hee Haw" and many from Goober – George Lindsay – who was his close friend. Also from Millie, the wife of my longtime friend and record promoter Mike Shepherd, was Grandpa's niece. One of my favorites concerns Grandpa having just been paid by a show promoter backstage. Grandpa kept counting and recounting his pay. On about the fourth count the promoter asked, "Well Grandpa, is it all there?" Grandpa finished counting, looked up and said "Just barely."

The dressing room closest to the stage at the Opry House was the biggest and was built for Roy Acuff. Mr. Acuff, as everyone called him, was a religious man and had a sign over the door. It read something like this, "There's nothing coming up today that the Lord and I can't handle." After he passed away, the dressing room was used by whoever was the host or headliner on any particular event. One night it was Willie and his band. As I walked by, the dressing room door opened and the floor was covered in empty beer cans and a cloud of smoke rolled out that made me think we should call the Fire Department. After having inhaled one time, all I wanted to do was find a big bag of Fritos.

I can't mention Mr. Acuff without telling this story. Late in his life, he lived in a house that was on the Opryland Theme Park property, very near the back door to the Grand Ole Opry and The Nashville Network's television studios. One night I was on Ralph Emery's popular "Nashville Now" TV show performing a song I recorded titled "Sex Symbols." I performed the song on stage during that time seated next to a life-sized dummy of Julio Iglesis. I manipulated the dummy's mouth and actions to his vocal part I recorded on a track to play in sync with the band. It was a pretty funny bit and it must have appeared very real to Mr. Acuff, who was watching the live broadcast from his home next door. Ralph told me the next day that Mr. Acuff had come over to the studio after my performance and wanted to shake hands with the famous Latin crooner.

Ralph said they told Mr. Acuff, whose eye sight must have been failing at that time, that he had just missed him, but would make sure he met Julio the next time he appeared. I'm just glad he didn't see him backstage folded up with his feet over his head in a travel trunk.

CHAPTER 13

Andy Williams and Barnaby Records

During the summer months, when network television shows took a break, it was customary to fill the show's time-slot with a replacement show designed to hold the audience until the new fall season. In 1970, the summer replacement for the top-rated "Andy Williams Show" was hosted by a scared to death young guy from Clarkdale, Georgia, named Ray Stevens. It was called "Andy Williams Presents The Ray Stevens Show" and the theme was "Who is Ray Stevens?"

The show was taped in Canada, and the writing-production teams later wrote and produced the "Sonny and Cher" and "Laugh-In" TV shows. One of the writers was a goofy guy named Steve Martin, who had not yet discovered his white suit. He did try out the fake arrow that went through his head, though. On my show, he wrote comedy and did skits from time to time. His zany approach fit right in with the overall mood of the show.

Even though I was scared to death, at the same time I was having the time of my life. I have admitted a number of times since that experience that I was not ready for it, but who is ever ready for something like that? Once a week you walk out in front of 20 to 30 million people and do your thing for an hour. In those days there was a good chance at least a third of those watching television in the United States and Canada were watching you because there was no cable and only three networks served up programming.

The best thing that came from that experience was a song I wrote after the producers said that they needed a theme song for the show. In Nashville, I lived in Camelot Acres, off Granny White Pike, at 5300 Lancelot Road, and had a music room downstairs. One day I told Penny and my two daughters, Timi and Suzi, to not bother me while I went into the basement music room to work. It was like that scene from *Young Frankenstein* where Gene Wilder says "No matter how I beg, don't open the door." I almost had to chain myself to the piano to make my manic self focus. I had never been in the position where I absolutely *had* to write anything before and I didn't have to but I felt that this was a unique opportunity. Inspiration for me had always been a pretty casual event and I had never been on anybody else's clock but my own. *No pressure!* All I had to do was write a great song worthy to be the theme for a prime time network TV show.

For three days I sat at the piano surrounded by wads of

paper with ideas that didn't work. I had done a lot of all-nighters where I wrote arrangements and string parts, the job of being purely creative was a different story. I tried everything: up tempo, down tempo, funny, showy, deep, light, serious, half-serious; everything!

I wanted to write a song that would say something like, "let's all be friends." Race relations were a big issue in those days. I had a little book of Chinese proverbs and, as I leafed through it, the phrase "everything is beautiful in its own way" caught my eye. I thought maybe that would work. The melody I constructed was a simple, repetitive pattern that led to the universally approved, philosophically perfect statement "everything is beautiful in its own way." It seemed to catch the mood of the time in our country. It was a notion that made everyone's head nod in agreement, everyone from Wall Street to Haight Ashbury, from Yuppies to Hippies.

There are several other songs by that title, because titles and ideas can't be copyrighted; otherwise there would be only one song in the world titled "I Love You." I have read that people claimed I took the melody from a famous French song, but I didn't. I had certainly heard the expression before, it was a fairly common one where I grew up. But, as with all works of art, several things came together to make something new. When I wrote and played "Everything is

Beautiful" for the first time, I knew I had the theme song for my show.

I recorded it at Cowboy Jack Clement's studio, and Charlie Tallent was the engineer. After we recorded it, I had the idea to go to the school where both my daughters attended and have the kids sing "Jesus loves the little children, all the little children of the world, red and yellow black and white, they are precious in his sight, Jesus loves the little children of the world" and add it to the beginning of the record, just before the chorus opened the song.

It was a hit. It's been recorded over 300 times around the world. It won a Grammy for me for "Male Vocalist of the Year." I was in Australia on tour when I won the Grammy, and I'm told that Glen Campbell accepted it for me.

"Everything Is Beautiful" established and broadened my career beyond anything I could have imagined. It took me around the world because it was a hit around the world. After that summer show on network television, the gates opened for live performances and I began to have a repertoire of recognizable hits that gave me a solid stage show with my own band. Don Williams used his many Las Vegas connections and William Morris began booking me there. We went to France, Great Britain, Germany and Australia. The doors were blown open for me by that exposure and "Everything is Beautiful" became a standard pop song.

Mike Shepherd played a big part in coordinating the promotion and marketing as it marched to the top of the charts and kept the pressing plants and distributors cranking out the records to feed the retail outlets. On every one of my network TV shows, I sang ... "Everything Is Beautiful" at the opening and close of the show. Barnaby Records was distributed by CBS, and the promotion staff and distribution of CBS played a major role in "Everything is Beautiful" becoming an international hit.

Mike loved working that record and told me that the highlight for him was a phone call he received from a lady who said that song had been instrumental in her husband returning to God, to her, and his family. We never know the impact of a song on the lives of people. "Everything Is Beautiful" had a powerful impact on mine. If it hadn't been for that song, I might have had to get that "real" job my daddy kept mentioning.

After "Everything is Beautiful," I had several more chart records and then recorded a gospel album where I played almost every instrument and sang every vocal part. Technology had progressed to the point where over-dubs did not create a lot of hiss, like they did in the old days. The great old Albert Brumley classic, "Turn Your Radio On," was a hit from that album and my recording of "Love Lifted Me" received a Grammy nomination. Next, I recorded a tribute to my adopted home town on the album *Nashville,* and had a crossover Pop/Country hit with it. Recently I re-recorded "Nashville" and put it on YouTube with a little video. It has received a lot of attention all over again over 40 years later.

My career as a Nashville session player was pretty much over because my career as a recording artist had eclipsed it. I moved from being a picker to being a personality, and that was uncomfortable for me. Like everyone, I like being known; identity is a driving force in all of us. When we meet someone new, we always want to know two things; what's your name and what do you do? However, the comfort of being known by a few talented and respected insiders for what you can do is a far cry from being known by strangers, even in foreign countries, for who you are. For some people, celebrity is a drug and they can't seem to get enough of it. Some people are famous today just for being famous. They don't seem to do or accomplish much of anything apart from achieving notoriety. As my talented friend Larry Gatlin sang, "Livin' in the spotlight can kill a man outright." We watch it daily and have tabloid papers and TV programs to chronicle the demise of the once glamorous and now fallen.

I opened a studio of my own on Grand Avenue and thought I wanted to be in the studio rental business. At that point, I was making good money and felt I needed to have some investments. The studio was really good, but the experience of letting other people use my studio and spill their coffee on the console and put out cigarettes on furniture did not contribute to my peace of mind. When a producer ran up a huge recording bill and stiffed me on it, the whole thing really turned sour so, I sold the studio. The one good thing that came out of that bad experience was a song I wrote as therapy for having been ripped off. "Mr. Businessman" turned out to be a hit.

Around this time I bought a small, old house on Music Row at 1707 Grand Avenue. I once overheard Chet Atkins say about me that "He's a beaver. He loves to build things" and, as I refurbished it, my beaver nature was in full swing. It was small but I had my own office, a reception area for a new employee, and a recording studio all my own. That little operation has grown to include half the block at the corner of 17th and Grand on Music Row, but the studio is still there and is near and dear to my heart because the first song I ever recorded there was "The Streak."

I had been in Los Angeles on one of my many trips to the coast in those days because my association with Don and "The Andy Williams Show" had opened many doors for me. I started using Tom Stasinis on Robertson Avenue, Andy's tailor, who was the tailor for a lot of Hollywood actors and

TV personalities. He made show clothes for me, as well as street clothes, for years. I'm a little hard to fit when it comes to trousers but Tom made perfect pants for me and I still have several pair.

On the plane returning from L.A., I read an article in an airline magazine about a campus phenomenon called "streaking," where college kids took off their clothes and ran naked across campuses at west coast colleges. I cut out the article and put it in my pocket, then began to think how this would go over in places less sophisticated than college campuses. As news about the pranks continued, I pulled out the article and, while sitting in my home in Camelot Acres, the line "They call him 'The Streak,' fastest thing on two feet" came to me. The idea was that there's this ole country boy who's not going for that business, but his wife is.

By the time we released "The Streak" on Barnaby Records, there were several other streaking records on the market but mine seemed to blow the others away or leave them in the dust. "Everything Is Beautiful" had set up the distributors for just what could happen with a Ray Stevens record, so everybody jumped on it from the get go and in four weeks Barnaby Records had sold five million of those little 45 RPM singles of "The Streak." Five million! It is unbelievable how fast those things sold and how much airplay that song got. It was the biggest record of the year all over this country, and in other countries as well. It was the biggest record of the year everywhere, that is, except at the Country Music Association. At the CMA Awards, the "Record of the Year" was awarded to "Country Bumpkin," a song by Cal Smith that was number one on the country charts for one week and stayed on the country chart for only ten weeks. I don't know the sales figures, but I'm quite sure it sold less than "The Streak."

I have not had a lot of disappointments in the music business, but failing to be recognized by my hometown organization after such an overwhelming success in the world-wide market place was rather disappointing. I never thought of Nashville as "Country Music City," and neither did Chet Atkins or Owen Bradley or most of the musicians. It's just "Music City" and it has always been about the music and not the label somebody else puts on it. I felt a little down about that snub, but in a few weeks the performance checks and the record sales statements starting landing in my mailbox and bank account, and it cheered me right up. Like Liberace once said, "I cried all the way to the bank!"

My tenure at Barnaby ended on a very high note. We were doing lots of TV shows back then, and I was booked regularly on afternoon talk shows like Merv Griffin, Mike

Douglas, and Dinah Shore, as well as network variety and music shows. One day we were rehearsing for one of those shows in my new recording studio, and during a break we started clowning around – as musicians often do – and used our country instrumentation as we played the jazz classic "Misty." It started sounding really good, so I slipped out and called the studio engineer and asked him to come over. After we finished rehearsing for the show, he set up microphones for everyone and, in a couple of takes, we recorded that song, which won a Grammy for "Best Arrangement of the Year." Good music is good music and a hit song will hold up no matter how you perform it. I later gave the same bluegrass treatment to another Pop/Rock standard "You Are So Beautiful" but "Misty" was the winner that I went out on at Barnaby.

Where did Andy Williams get the name Barnaby for his record label, you might ask? It was named for a dog he had as a kid.

CHAPTER 14

Music Publishing and Real Estate

After I moved into my new studio and offices at 1707 Grand Avenue in the early 1970s, I hired a secretary, Shirley Welch, but Shirley Ruth, or "Ms. Ruth," was much more than a secretary. Shirley had worked for the Grand Ole Opry, for Hubert Long, an old time Nashville talent manager, and music business man and legendary songwriter, Harlan Howard. She knew the music business inside out and upside down. I was not happy with the accounting firm that Don Williams hooked me up with on the west coast, primarily because they were on the west coast and had gotten me involved in California laws. Chet and Owen, my heroes, had always done business with Joe Kraft, an accountant in Nashville, so I sought him out. Joe had a wonderful, steady paternal manner and took care of getting me out of California and back into Tennessee. He set up my publishing and other interests in a very manageable and economical manner.

I had been acquiring real estate on Music Row and since Joe represented both Chet and me, we started buying property together. I always liked the idea of owning real estate. When I acquired some money, I looked around and thought, "What are the guys who are successful doing with their money?" I looked at Chet, Owen, and Eddy Arnold, and saw that they all owned real estate. I met Park Owen who was, at that time, the premiere real estate salesman with Dobson-Johnson in Nashville and he called me whenever he saw a good deal. That's how I started buying old houses on Music Row.

Music is not the only business in Music City. I was no longer a session player, except on my own recordings, but was a writer, publisher, performer, producer, and Music Row property owner. The Kraft brothers and Nina Sivak worked hand-in-hand with Shirley to take care of my interests, pay my taxes, and look after my backside so I could attend to my creative work with full confidence that "somethin' wasn't gainin' on me," as Satchel Paige once warned.

A lot of people had been re-recording songs that I had released but there were more good songs around Nashville than I could ever get around to recording on my own, so I took a lesson from Bill Lowery and developed a publishing catalog. My brother, John Ragsdale, worked with me while attracting writers, making demos, and pitching songs and we had success with cuts by Brenda Lee, Jerry Lee Lewis, the Captain and Tennille, Elvis, and others. John is a steady hand and knew everyone in town. He did a great job of representing me and my interests, as he always has.

In 1971, I signed Layng Martine, a young songwriter from the New York area, who came to town to write and be a star. Layng had a song, "Rub It In," about asking a girl to rub suntan lotion on him. I published it, recorded him singing it, and released it on Barnaby with Mike Shepherd working the record. It went to number 65 on the charts and did pretty well, but two years later Billy "Crash" Craddock recorded it and took it all the way to Number One. But that's not the best part. A few years later the giant firm Johnson and Johnson had a new product called "plug-ins" which was a new kind of air freshener. They licensed that song for their advertising campaign, but changed "rub it in" to "plug it in." They renewed that agreement for several years until the radio and TV commercials generated more income than the record sales and airplay performances.

Layng wrote and I published "Way Down," the last song Elvis recorded, which was his hit on the radio at the time he died. It has been a great copyright. Layng established his own publishing company shortly after that, and it has pleased me to see how well he has done. He was recently inducted into the Nashville Songwriters Hall of Fame.

Old "Tex" Davis knew something when he advised Bill

Lowery to start a music publishing company. I now have four of them. My original company, Ahab Music Publishing, Inc., is affiliated with the performance licensing organization BMI, Ray Stevens Music is also a BMI affiliate, Grand Avenue Music is affiliated with ASCAP, and Lucky Streak Music is with SESAC.

Sometime around 1975, I came home from a series of road shows and Shirley told me that an old acquaintance had stopped by and dropped off a tape of new material for me to listen to; he was looking for a publisher. It was Buddy Kalb, Big Buddy K, from the Lowery days in Atlanta, but I had lost track of him over the years. He had given up music in favor of a day job at the Ford Motor Company during the mid-sixties, but was beginning to write again. He left me three songs and I liked them all, which is very unusual for me or anybody else in the music business. Great songs are hard to find. I recorded all of those songs and since that day I have recorded over 120 he has written and have published between 300 and 400 more; many have been recorded by other artists.

Buddy moved to Nashville in the late eighties and helped with my publishing companies, video production, and TV direct marketing campaigns and looked after my Nashville operation during those years I was in Branson. He has been my co-writer, consultant and friend for the last 40 years. We work together every day.

Chet Atkins was a great instrumental recording artist. One of the great honors I received came when Chet asked me to produce him on some records where he sang. I produced "Frog Kissin'," a song that Buddy wrote that was later recorded by George Burns and several others. I also produced a session on Minnie Pearl doing old R and B songs like "Mama He Treats Your Daughter Mean" and "Tweedly Dee."

In addition to being a great songwriter, Buddy also found a couple of hit songs for my publishing companies. "Cadillac Style" and "I Can't Reach Her Anymore," both recorded by Sammy Kershaw, were written by Mark Peterson, who was a guitarist on the Shotgun Red show for several years. You never know when or where you will come across a Hit song. Everybody thinks they have written one, but trust me – it's not all that easy. I wrote a song the other day and someone asked me how long it took me to write it. I told him, "60 years."

CHAPTER 15

The Nashville Sound

C het Atkins was a dear friend and real estate business partner, as well as one of the greatest producers to ever record in Nashville. He was a real Music Business Man and I learned a lot from him both in and out of the studio. He produced hits on acts such as Don Gibson, the Everly Brothers, Skeeter Davis, The Browns, Hank Snow, and Eddy Arnold. Owen Bradley was the other great producer who helped establish Nashville as "Music City U.S.A.," but Chet and Owen were different in their approaches to producing. Owen knew the sound he wanted and, when he found it, he stuck with it. The artists he signed fit that sound. That became known as "The Nashville Sound" and Owen used the great "A Team" musicians. Chet used them too, but Chet also hired off-the-wall musicians who put a splash of color on sessions.

Chet was the "King" of the Nashville music business from the 1950s through the 1970s. He was an outstanding multi-Grammy winning musician, known all over the world for his unique style of finger picking that was inspired by Merle Travis. Chet's style was different than Merle's because, while both used their thumbs, Travis used only his index finger, while Chet included his two middle fingers. He developed that style because he couldn't see how Travis played when he heard him on the radio and he thought he was copying him.

I can't over-emphasize the importance and the impact that Chet and Owen had on the music of their era, and for years to come. They were the King-Pins of the Nashville music scene.

I played on a number of sessions for Chet and receiving his approval, and getting the opportunity to work with him was the chance of a lifetime. Chet was both a Star and Star-Maker in Nashville, and when young guys from Georgia, like Ray Stevens and Jerry Reed, received support and encouragement from him, it was like being dubbed a "Knight" by "The King." It meant instant acceptance in the elite little club of musicians, writers, and producers that was Nashville in those days. It was a ticket to the inner circle. Few received such an acceptance and the two of us who did, Jerry Reed and me, are a testament to the generosity of Chet Atkins. He was comfortable making a place for the talent of others, and equally comfortable saying, "That's turr-able" when something wasn't so good. Whenever a famous guitar player would come to town, they always wanted to meet Chet, Mr. Guitar, but what they didn't know or could hardly believe was that Chet wanted to meet them to hear and watch them play and see what he could learn. People called him a Master of the Guitar and he was, but he was also the greatest student of the instrument that I ever met. There's never been anyone like him and probably never will be again.

Chet and I became close friends. We often played golf together – we were both members of the Hillwood Country Club – and one day we were both in a golf cart with me driving when I made a quick turn and Chet fell out of the cart. He didn't speak to me for several holes. He never let me drive the golf cart after that, and when we went to lunch he would try to arrange it so that someone else drove. (Usually Harry Warner, a mutual friend who worked at BMI).

CHAPTER 16

Comedian of the Year?

Televised awards shows have become a part of the national music and entertainment scene for every genre. They recently announced the new YouTube Music Awards Show. It won't be long, I guess, before they will have the "Singing in the Shower" Awards. At one time there was just the Oscars, and that show drew such an audience that TV producers everywhere started creating awards shows for everything: Grammy's, People's Choice, CMA, ACM, Best Tattoo and Tongue Stud, and on and on. I've done all kinds of awards shows through the years and have tried to keep my appearances fresh. One year I rode down the aisle of the theatre and up onto the stage on a Harley motorcycle during the time my song "Shriner's Convention" was on the charts, and on another show I had a U.F.O. land on the stage and three pink Martians came out of it to dance with me. That was for the song "I Saw Elvis in a U.F.O." Once on a show hosted by the talented singer Janie Fricke, I wrote a song to sing to her, "Janie Fricke, I'm Gonna Give You a Hickey."

At one time the Music City News Awards was the Country Music biggie, and it was later merged with The Nashville Network to create the TNN/Music City News Awards Show broadcast from Nashville. As I have said before, folks in media have never known what to do with me when it comes to putting me in a category or niche. Because I do a lot of comedy songs, that awards show classified me as a Comedian and as such, I won their Comedian of the Year Award nine years in a row. Not bad for a piano player. I do a little stand-up comedy during my shows. Actually, I call it sit-down comedy because I do it mostly from the piano bench, but nevertheless the audience seems to like the jokes as much as they do the songs in my show, and if I change them or leave one out they heard before, they get upset. "I brought my Dad to hear the Dog Joke and you didn't do it!" Folks can be peculiar; they will complain when you do the same stuff over and over, and then complain when you don't. But mostly they laugh and applaud (thankfully).

My sit-down routines are folksy and about family members, but my family doesn't mind; they've gotten used to it. My mother didn't really mind when I told folks she was such a bad cook that all the flies in Clarkdale chipped in to fix the hole in our screen door, or that it was rumored that South American Indians used to travel all the way to Georgia just to dip their arrows in her gravy. She was always good natured about my jokes but she did have a way of saying things in a convoluted way that was often confusing. Like one day when I was climbing a tree in the backyard, she yelled out the back door, "Now don't you fall out of that tree and break both your legs and come running to me!"

When I tell people that I came from a big family, a family that was so big that I didn't sleep by myself until I got married, they seem to understand.

I always mention my cousin Doris and her husband, and the fact that they have nine kids. I point out that they would have had ten but they read somewhere that every tenth child born in America is Hispanic – and neither of them could speak Spanish. Actually, the real reason they had so many kids is because Doris is slightly deaf. Every night when they were getting ready for bed, her husband would ask, "Hey Doris, you want to watch TV or what?" Doris always answered, "What?"

The family member who gets the most laughs is my old Grandpa. I tell how he is so forgetful that we have to feed him an extra portion of beans when we go camping so we can find him in case he wanders off into the woods. He really is forgetful. He went to the Doctor last week, and during the examination the Doctor discovered a suppository in his ear. When he told Grandpa what he found, Grandpa asked to use the phone. The Doctor asked him why he needed a phone, and he said he wanted to call Grandma and tell her that he thought he knew now where he had put his hearing aid. I know it's an old joke, but sometimes old jokes are like old friends or an old dog – kind of comforting. Besides, there are two elements to humor – you can either tell a funny joke, or you can tell a joke funny. And jokes are like food – you may have eaten the same meal numerous times, but presentation can make a lot of difference.

Before we leave Grandpa, I have to tell you about the time he went on the road with me. I was going to do a show in Miami Beach and when I asked if he wanted to go along, he jumped at the chance. Funny, he turned down a trip with me to Fargo, North Dakota, just the week before. Anyway, we got to Miami and had just checked into this beautiful high rise beach-front hotel, and I was unpacking my bag when the phone rang. It was the desk clerk and he informed me that we had to check out. When I said, "What's wrong? We just checked in," he just said, "It's your grandfather!" I said, "What'd he do?" and the clerk said that he had wet the pool. I started thinking fast and said, "Wait a minute, are you trying to tell me that in this big 500-room hotel with all these kids running around, that my Grandfather is the only one who wet the pool?" The desk clerk said, "No, Mr. Stevens, but he is the only one who wet if from the high dive."

I've been doing that kind of humor along with my songs for the last 50 years, and people are as fond of some of those jokes as they are for the million selling hit songs. But the story that gets the biggest reaction and most laughs by far is the one I tell about my Grandma and her "problem." I can't share it with you, it's one of those things where you have to be there. Hey, I just remembered – I told that story during a show that was taped and made available on DVD titled *Ray Stevens Such a Night....50 Years of Hits and Hilarity.* So you can buy that DVD and hear it, or you can wait until I come to your area and come see me in person.

CHAPTER 17

Warner Brothers-R.C.A Victor-MCA

I moved to Nashville in 1962, and the major record companies began to move their office operations and staffs for country music to Music City during the 1960s as well. Most settled on Music Row when they came here. Later, Capitol Records built a beautiful building on the Row on a piece of property that Chet and I sold them, but they never moved into it. The gospel record label and publisher, Word Records, is in that building. Capitol moved a couple of miles away and rented space in a high-rise building on West End Avenue at Murphy Road before the company was sold to Universal Music. That operation is now located downtown, next to the Ryman Auditorium. After 60 years, the major labels are beginning to move away from Music Row, and many of them are merging.

Decca Records became MCA, then became Universal and they left Music Row for those downtown offices. RCA and CBS Records were both acquired by Sony, and that company is located on 18th Avenue South, part of the Music Row community, but no longer on Music Row like they once were. Warner Brothers is still on Music Row in a building they built for their record company. What used to be six major labels – RCA, CBS, Capitol, Warner Brothers, Polygram/Mercury, and MCA – is at this writing down to three. That happened after Napster came in with their free downloading, and sales of recordings dropped to half of what they were during a twelve year period from 2000 to 2012.

I've known most of the record company executives over the years and have been signed by many of them. In my recording career, I started out on Prep, a subsidiary of Capitol, then on Capitol (the parent label) after Prep folded, then on the Lowery-owned company NRC. I have been signed as an artist to Mercury, Monument, Barnaby, Warner Brothers, RCA Victor, MCA, Capitol/Curb for one release and then Curb, and finally my own label, Clyde Records. Someone recently asked why a person changed labels and the answer is that you either get romanced away by a label who promises to give you a better deal and promises more exposure for you, or you leave on your own with the same hope.

During my years at Warner Brothers and RCA Victor, I made a lot of records that I liked but only a few of them were hits. "Honky Tonk Waltz" was written by Paul Craft, who later wrote "It's Me Again Margaret" for me at MCA.

I recorded "You Are So Beautiful" bluegrass style, and did the Glenn Miller big band classic "In the Mood" as a hen house full of clucking chickens, rather than saxophones and trombones, under the name "The Henhouse Five Plus Too." That recording received a lot of radio airplay and I have heard that many low-watt daytime-only radio stations across rural America used it to sign on with every morning. Later, I did the chicken thing again on "Thus Spake Zarathustra" by Richard Strauss. That song is better known as the opening theme for the movie *2001 A Space Odyssey,* and was also the song that brought Elvis on stage for years. It's very dramatic, but I thought the chickens were a nice touch.

When I joined RCA Victor, I recorded an album and a song that continues to receive a lot of attention at my concerts. The idea came when I played a show in Atlanta, and we had an early flight the next morning to go to our next gig. We had planned on a good night's sleep in a nice hotel before our early morning flight, but the Shriners' were holding a convention at the same hotel and they had other plans. Those plans were to keep everyone in the hotel up all night with them.

It sounded like they had motorcycles in the hallways and when I looked out my window at the pool area around three in the morning, there was a motorcycle down there with a group of Shriners still going strong. The Shriners sure know how to party hearty. They are professionals.

It was a long, sleepless night, and on the flight the next morning I slowly began to see the humor in it and started putting a song together. I performed "Shriner's Convention" on a televised music awards show that year and opened the show by riding a Harley down through the audience and up on the stage. Jim Owens was the producer of that show and later I worked with his video production crew to produce some very successful videos. Jim is married to Lorianne Crook of Crook and Chase T.V. show fame.

I had another chart single on RCA, "Night Games," written by Buddy Kalb, that went to the top 20. After that, I went back to Mercury for a one-album deal and released an album titled "Me" that had the single "My Dad" that charted. That song wasn't a big hit, but it has always been a favorite of mine.

After RCA, I re-joined MCA in the early '80s and things got pretty interesting. There were creative people at MCA in their "Special Products" division who wanted to try direct response TV advertising. They compiled a two-album package, *Get the Best of Ray Stevens,* and I worked with them to produce the TV ads. It was a joint venture where I shared some risk in consideration for added reward if the offer was successful.

The TV spots were a hit and MCA sold over 500,000 double album sets – a million vinyl discs and cassette tapes. That was pretty impressive and that was just TV; there were additional follow up sales in catalogs and at retail outlets. This started me thinking seriously about television advertising. I had seen the fast talking TV ads for Slim Whitman, Boxcar Willie, Zamphir the Pan Flute Phenomenon of Europe, and others, but when I saw the sales numbers generated by my two-album set, I began to take this marketing direction much more seriously.

Fred Keir was from Chicago and had been hired by MCA to produce the TV spots, so I contacted him directly and proposed a project of twenty saxophone standards played by Boots Randolph, a long-time friend and label mate from the Monument days. I produced the twenty sides and we sold the albums on TV and, I must say, we did quite well. We made money and I learned a lot about the direct sales business that paid off later. Meanwhile, I had a resurgence in record sales and radio airplay from my first album released on MCA through traditional channels. That album was *He Thinks He's Ray Stevens* and, on the cover, I'm dressed as Napoleon. I have to believe that it was the TV exposure that stirred the audience interest in me again.

One of the hits on that album, "It's Me Again

Margaret," was written by Paul Craft. I had kept his original recording of that song in my desk drawer for years trying to figure out how to produce a song about an obscene phone caller that did not creep out every woman in America. Finally, I said "what the hell" and recorded the funniest record I could. There was a little negative flack, but very little – and nothing compared to the overwhelming positive response that record received. People had yelled "Shut up Baby I'm trying to sing" at me in public for years because of "Gitarzan," and then "Don't Look Ethel" when they saw me because of that line in "The Streak". But now I began to hear "Are You Nekkid?" everywhere I went. One day, walking down an aisle at Wal-Mart, I passed a woman pushing a grocery cart with a small child, about three years old, in the kiddie seat. We had passed each other and I was about twenty feet down the aisle when I heard this little voice cry out "Are you Nekkid?" I turned around and saw that little kid leaning out from that kiddie seat, looking around his Mama at me! I've been told that kiddies have yelled it out in Sunday School before. It's nice to know you are having an influence on the youth of America.

The surprise hit from that album was "Mississippi Squirrel Revival," and that song started happening when a disc jockey on a Rock'n'Roll station in Jackson, Mississippi, began playing it every hour. The famous news commentator, Paul Harvey, also heard it and talked about it on his daily 15-minute radio broadcast that was syndicated on hundreds of country radio stations all over the country. It was never a hit on all the radio stations in the country at the same time, but it remained on the air for months because, after it peaked in the Southeast, stations in the Southwest started playing it and then the Mid-West picked it up. At the end of that year both "It's Me Again, Margaret" and "The Mississippi Squirrel Revival" were nominated for "Comedy/Novelty Song of the Year."

"Mississippi Squirrel Revival" was written by Buddy Kalb with help from his wife, Carlene, so I was pleased when Buddy and Carlene were called to the stage and picked up the award on national TV. That began a run of awards for me as I picked up my first award for "Comedian of the Year." As I mentioned earlier, I made that same trip to the stage every year for the next nine years to receive that award. I have them all in a row in my office to remind me that I'm supposed to be a Comedian. Well, maybe.

During the rest of the eighties, I recorded six albums for MCA and we had a wonderful run of success. One song I recorded, "Would Jesus Wear A Rolex on His Television Show," was written by my old friend Chet Atkins with Margaret Archer. Margaret is a talented singer who played around town with a group called The Cluster Pluck-ers for several years. That song was released during the scandals connected with televangelists Jim and Tammy Bakker and Jimmy Swaggart. It received a lot of publicity and even garnered a Grammy nomination. I have received 12 of those over the years.

During those years on MCA my records received a lot of radio play, TV nominations and awards, and enabled me to work all the road dates I wanted. I was drawing good crowds, the concert promoters were making profits, and my price for personal appearances kept climbing. I headlined in Las Vegas at the Desert Inn and acts such as Lynda Carter, known on TV as "Wonder Woman," Louise Mandrell, Janie Fricke, Tanya Tucker and The Smoth-ers Brothers. During that run of shows, my organization produced opening video segments and we did shows with themes like "Ethel Gets Kidnapped" or "Agent 006 ½," which gave the show some continuity.

The segments went over well when I played in Las Vegas. They also went over well when I did shows in Branson, a little town in southwest Missouri.

CHAPTER 18

Dog Jokes

O ops! I forgot to mention the Dog Jokes. People love dogs. There's just something that is so optimistic and forgiving and lovable about them. I saw a little plaque the other day that said "I'd like to be the man that my dog thinks I am."

I have had several dogs in my life and I've sung about them and talked about them in my shows for years. Once I had a Bull Mastiff that was so big, he lived on Pot Roast and Pomeranians. His name was Deefer. That's 'D' fer dog. Clever, huh? I'm just kidding about the Pomeranians; he was actually a sweetheart. The only thing you had to worry about was him sitting on you and slobbering.

I have told a series of jokes through the years about dogs in my shows that people remember, and ask for like they were songs. As my act grew and developed, the Dog Jokes became very popular everywhere from Fair dates to Las Vegas to Branson. They are really dumb, but I'll share some of them with you here because if I don't, someone will complain that I left them out.

I once went to a kennel and asked if they had a blind dog. The man asked, "Do you mean a seeing eye dog?" I told him, No, that I actually needed a blind dog because it was for my mother-in-law and if the dog ever got a look at her he would go for her throat. He said he didn't have a blind dog but that he did have a deaf dog that he could sell me. I thought about it for a minute and decided if the dog didn't have to listen to my mother-in-law then he might leave her alone, so I bought him. He was exactly as the man had said, deaf as a post. I started feeling sorry for him so I went out and bought a little hearing aid for him. I put it in his ear, duct taped a battery pack around his tummy and when I flipped that switch to "ON" he froze, perked up both his ears and cocked his head from side to side. He was hearing sounds for the first time, like crickets chirping and birds singing. He got so excited that he ran around the house several times, ran up to a tree, raised his leg and electrocuted himself! Can you believe it?

If you can, you might believe the story about the dog I had when we first moved to Nashville. We were so poor back then that we had only one bedroom, no spare tire and my dog only had three legs. I called him "Tripod." Every time he ran up to a tree, he would just fall over. So I bought him a little peg leg. As you might have guessed, I buy a lot of stuff at the handicapped pet store. He learned to walk on that little peg leg really well, but one day he got in a grass fire and burned to the ground.

After that, I had a dog with no legs at all, so I didn't bother to name him. I mean, if you called him, he wouldn't come anyway. He was a lot of fun though and every day I would take him for a drag. He loved it when it snowed. I taught him how to do tricks too, like roll over. That was easy, but one day he did it on a hill and I never saw him again.

We often play Casinos and Supper Clubs with themes, and they always identify their restrooms according to the theme. Like we performed in one by the sea and the restrooms were Bouys and Gulls. One time we played a Sportsman's Club and the restrooms were named for hunting dogs but it was confusing for me because I didn't know if I was a Pointer or a Setter. I mean I know what I am – I just didn't know what those dogs were – so I accidently walked into the Setters. And there they were – setting. They were surprised and I was shocked. I was shocked to see that there was much more graffiti in the Women's restrooms than in the Men's. It confused me until I had a chance to think about it. I mean, after all, they do have both hands free.

I had been playing at my own theatre in Branson, and the word was out about our sold-out shows and record crowds. It was also about the time that my face was all over TV with those commercials for the *Comedy Video Classics* video tape and everyone assumed that I was rolling in dough. I was home in Nashville during the Christmas hiatus between seasons and went to lunch with Chet Atkins at a popular restaurant called the Nashville Country Club. When we walked in, it was packed – and sitting all the way in the back was Jimmy Dean at a table with several Nashville music business types. When Dean saw us walk in the front door, he said in his Texas voice that could be heard from Dallas to Ft. Worth, "There's that Raaaay Stevens. He's so rich he's going to buy his dog a boy for Christmas!"

Grandpa Jones told the story of a Pit Bull that ran up to him and grabbed him around the knee with his front paws and started doing what dogs are prone to do. When Grandpa sort of kicked and told him firmly to "Get Away!," the Pit Bull snarled and showed his teeth, so Grandpa said, "Well, OK, hurry up then."

CHAPTER 19

Branson Calling

Branson had long been an Ozark Mountain vacation destination for people who wanted to fish or see fall colors when the air got chilly and the trees turned. Years before I ever played in Branson, a popular book was written about the region titled *Shepherd of the Hills*. That book had been a best seller and was made into a popular film starring a young John Wayne. Before I arrived in Branson, that small town was booming with several music theaters that showcased the talents of local families like "The Presleys," "The Plummers," "The Brashlers," and the Cabe family, who billed themselves "The Baldnobbers" after a mountain, and a group from the *Shepherd of the Hills* novel.

Jim Thomas, a concert promoter in Branson, had enticed Roy Clark to lend his name to a theater there where Roy worked a few dates each year. The rest of the schedule was filled with other Nashville acts. I had worked there pretty regularly and was drawing sellout crowds. In 1990, as I was putting together my tour schedule for the next year,

I asked Jim how many dates he wanted me to do in 1991. It was a total shock when he answered, "How about all of them?" I hesitated for a moment and then said, "Can I get back to you on that?"

I knew Jim Thomas as an honorable promoter and an excellent businessman. He knew the Branson market and if he was ready to roll the dice on Ray Stevens for a whole season, then maybe Ray Stevens should roll those dice himself. It could be very lucrative but, most importantly, I would have the chance to build something really big, like a theater. My Beaver nature was intrigued with the idea.

When I became aware of what was going on in Branson, with all their performance theaters for entertainment, I thought it would be a natural for Nashville. I had tried to get people in Nashville interested in developing a the-ater-based destination for Country and Pop music, but it seemed like no one had a vision that reached beyond the Grand Ole Opry and the Opryland Hotel.

There were only a couple of places where a hit artist could play in Nashville, other than the downtown arena. There was the Grand Ole Opry House and the Opryland Hotel Complex, The Acuff Theatre, located on the same property, and the Ryman Auditorium, the former home of the Grand Ole Opry. People from all across the coun-try and around the world believed they could come to

Nashville and see and/or hear their favorite artists performing at any number of venues every night. However, the real Nashville didn't work that way. That concept was actually only available in Branson at that time. Nashville had a lot of small club-type venues where new artists and writers showcased their material, and that is a uniquely Nashville experience. But to make money performing, an artist always has to leave town. Acts perform on the Grand Ole Opry Show as advertising for their out of town performances.

I wanted to see that change. When I was offered an entire season at the Roy Clark Theater in Branson by Jim Thomas, I thought why not produce something like that here in Nashville? Branson was difficult to get to from Nashville. It is a seven and a half hour steady drive with only about two of those hours on an interstate highway and the airline connections were a joke. It took as long to fly there as it did to drive. If I were going to Branson to play for an extended period of time, I was going to have to live there for an extended period of time and I did not like that option. I reasoned that if I built a theater, or rented a theater in Nashville, I could sleep in my own bed every night, which is my custom. Also, I have interests other than performing. I make records, oversee several pieces of commercial real estate, and run four publishing companies, in addition to making an attempt to write a song or two of my own from time to time. A place to play in Nashville seemed like a much sweeter deal. Nashville is my home, after all.

I tried to find a venue or a piece of property to develop. I met with people in government and with the Chamber of Commerce. The bottom line was that everyone acted as though what I talked about was some kind to threat to Opryland, rather than an expansion of the Nashville music franchise that would benefit everyone. Car dealers had figured out a long time ago that if they all located on the same side of town they would all benefit from each other's advertising and traffic. High tide raises all the boats, so to speak.

There is no doubt that the advertising dollars spent by Opryland would draw lots of people who, after attending Opryland, would become aware of other theaters and entertainment opportunities – but the reverse would be true as well. The Opryland philosophy was simple: Get people to town and house them in their hotel on their property and don't give them any reason to leave their property until they returned home.

To put it mildly, my idea of a theater complex similar to the ones in Branson was not well received. If I were going to attempt such a thing in Nashville, I would be on my own. I wanted to see the performance side of the music business flourish here in Nashville and was ready to buy property and build buildings, but there was simply no enthusiasm for that idea. It was a business I would have liked to been involved with in Nashville, but it was not to be.

In the ensuing years, a problem developed with the infrastructure in Branson. It isn't a big town – in fact it is very small. When you drive to Branson and get on Highway 76, Country Music Boulevard, you pass every theatre as you creep along in the traffic, and boy is there traffic! People flocked to this town and they all wanted to go to the same place at the same time and there was just one way to get there and one way to get back. Back when I started there, The Roy Clark Theater hosted a series of Nashville acts every couple of weeks. In addition, all the hillbilly family shows I mentioned were there, and then Boxcar Willie and Jim Stafford were regulars. Mel Tillis had rented a theatre for his show and was doing great business.

The popularity of Branson and the resistance in Nashville made it pretty clear what I needed to do, although several people around me were against it. I have good people working with me who are free to speak their minds about the pros and cons of any new idea. They had seen me on the road for three and four week runs and wondered out loud how I could possibly spend that many months away from Nashville. I heard what they were saying and I also knew the risk, but something kept tugging at me. Larry McFaden, an old friend who had been the bass player in Mel Tillis's band for years and later became the manager of Lee Greenwood and publisher of his songs like "God Bless the U.S.A.," was a strong advocate of my move to Branson and offered to be an investor. Gary Snaden, who owned the "Shepherd of the Hills" outdoor theatre attraction in Branson also owned a piece of property at the corner of Highway 76 and Shepherd of the Hills Expressway that was perfect for the site of a theater, and he also wanted to be a partner.

Joe Kraft and I formed a Missouri corporation, Ahab of the Ozarks, with McFaden and Snaden as partners, and I owned 51 percent in the deal. We hired an architect, went to work and were ready for a grand opening in June, 1991. In less than six months we built a theatre, equipped it, decorated it, staffed it, hired musicians, wrote a show, built special props, rehearsed, and were ready to do two shows a day, six days a week. My brother, John, handled my concessions business on the road for the previous two or three years and did a great job selling merchandise during and after the shows. He became the Master of Ceremonies for the Branson show and, when I sang "Gitarzan," he was in the gorilla suit and swung out on stage on a vine. John eventually took over the gift shop in the lobby as well as the in-theatre concessions like tapes, t-shirts, and caps, etc.

We found a great theatre manager, Mike Hughes, and Christina, a bus booker who soon became Christina Hughes, and a staff of dedicated people who pitched in like it was their own theatre. They were wonderful. I could write a book sometime about that experience and all of those people. I still hear from many of them and they all contributed to the success of "The Ray Stevens Theatre" experience in Branson.

During those years, I performed for over 1.6 million paying customers over a period of twenty months. In addition to show tickets, we sold cassettes, VHS tapes, t-shirts, sweat shirts, magnets, cups, earrings, and Lord only knows what all. We were the number one beverage dispenser in town and also sold hot dogs, along with popcorn and candy. It was like a toll booth on an eight-lane highway to paradise. We actually had to build more seats before the second year, and add more rest rooms to accommodate all of the paying customers. But that's not the most important thing we did between the first and second seasons.

A concession item that sold incredibly well was a VHS video tape we compiled from the videos I had done at MCA and Curb Records, along with video material from a Vegas show opening. I was skeptical about offering a VHS with such small content for sale. "Who's gonna buy that when it cost twenty bucks?" I asked myself. The answer, at the end of that first season, was "Almost everybody!" So, during the hiatus between seasons we shot four more videos to add to the package to give it more value for the $20 price tag, and we also made TV commercials for it. Working with Gary Wetter from California at WnR Direct, we decided to run those TV ads and capitalize on our experience with the MCA record offer and the Boots Randolph TV offer experience. What happened next was a phenomenon and deserves more room than I have left here.

CHAPTER 20

A Comedy Video Classic

Branson was a smash and at the end of that first year I was tired, but energized by the success. We closed the theatre in early November, 1991, and planned to open again in late spring, 1992. In the meantime, I had a lot to do. First, there was a lot of business and just plain normal living to catch up on back in Nashville. Two shows a day, six days a week for five and a half months had taken its toll. I bought a condo in Branson at the Pointe Royal Golf Course and before I went over, I planned to build a recording studio in the theatre. I originally thought that I would do the two shows, play a little golf and might make some records over there as well. The reality was that I went to bed every night after midnight, got up and showered, dressed, ate and was at the theatre by noon. I got on the phone and took care of some Nashville business and then took care of some theatre business before the first show started at 2 p.m. That show was over by 4:15 and the parking lot cleared out by 5 o'clock, which gave me time to freshen up, have dinner somewhere and, after fighting the traffic, return by seven for the last show at 8 pm. That did not leave much time for golf or recording or anything else.

In that first off-season, we changed the hours of the shows from 2 p.m. and 8 p.m., to 3 p.m. and 8 p.m. That helped a little, but still didn't give me any time for anything but doing the shows. On Sundays that first year we drove to Springfield, about 40 miles up the road, to find something to eat other than Mom and Pop food. We had to drive that far to get something as sophisticated as an Olive Garden. That changed during the next two years because the town began to boom. My manager, Don Williams, invited his brother, Andy, out to see what was happening. As a result, Andy purchased land and built his own Moon River Theatre there. A few other artists did the same thing.

During that first break, I contacted Jim Owens, whose Nashville organization produced a couple of my videos as well as a TV pilot, "Ray Stevens Amazing Rolling Revue" that we shot for The Nashville Network. The show offered a novel approach for a Comedy/Variety show that my brother John, Buddy, and I had developed whereby we pretended that I had a theatre inside an R.V. The opening showed people lining up and entering a 24 foot R.V., but they actually entered a cafe setting with a stage and lights. Darrell Waltrip, the famous NASCAR driver and good friend, was on the show as the driver of the camper and we pretended to drive all over town to cover breaking news events like Elvis being spotted at a Burger King in a U.F.O. that went through the drive-thru.

It was a funny concept and came off well, but TNN was looking for a standard variety show where people walked out, sang, and then walked off. I had been offered that deal for years but wanted to do something different. I wanted to shoot more videos and add them to the video package we sold at the theatre so we could have a package that offered customers a better value. I also wanted to offer the product on television with the "Amazing Rolling Revue" as a bonus, or "up-sell" as it's called by folks who do that sort of thing.

I wanted to make TV commercials for the video package using the funniest bits from each, which is what I observed was done with movie trailers. I would see a TV commercial for a funny movie, but when I got to the movie I often found that I had already seen the funniest stuff on the TV commercial. We didn't have that problem because we had eight videos but only 45 seconds to show funny stuff – and we had lots and lots of funny stuff. We made a short commercial and a long one. The short one was 45 seconds of clips and then a blue screen came on with the address, phone number, and a guy talking a mile a minute imploring viewers to "order now." The staff at Jim Owens

Productions helped us edit the commercials, as well as videos for "The Streak," "Everything is Beautiful," "Mississippi Squirrel Revival," and "It's Me Again Margaret."

Gary Wetter in Los Angeles had been involved in most of the successful TV offers of the day and, along with Rollie Froelich, a guy in Nashville with a shipping facility, we set up an 800 number. West Telemarketing established a banking and credit card processing operation. We arranged for reputable manufacturing, and we put *Ray Stevens Comedy Video Classics* on TV in the early spring before we went back to Branson for the 1992 season.

I am fortunate to be surrounded by people who are willing and capable of doing just about anything. My organization was in the business of sending me all around the country with five or six musicians doing as many as one hundred shows a year, in addition to recording an album a year while looking over my real estate interests and publishing. Shirley Welch was my secretary/assistant, my brother John took care of concessions, and Buddy oversaw everything. Then we built, staffed, and equipped a theatre operation, produced and marketed a TV product on a nationwide campaign, as well as ran the record company that produced the product. None of us had ever done anything like that before. We launched and managed two multi-million dollar operations from scratch at the same time. We had help, but we were the heart of the teams that were put together to make it happen.

Ray Stevens Comedy Video Classics sold 2.1 million video cassettes. *The Amazing Rolling Revue,* that we offered as an up-sell, sold over 250,000 more. The "Classics" sold for $19.95 plus $4.95 shipping and handling, and the "Amazing Rolling Revue" sold for $12.95 more. "Classics" was named the "Direct Response Product of the Year" and *Billboard* magazine voted it "Video of the Year." The television commercials were omnipresent, thanks to Gary Wetter.

Turner Broadcasting used the commercials on a co-op basis or what they call P.I.'s for "payment per inquiry." That meant that instead of us paying for the commercials that aired, we shared the revenue with Turner Broadcasting when they broadcast Atlanta Braves baseball games nationwide. Ted Turner called the Braves "The Nation's Team" and during rain delays Turner ran all of the spots that advertisers paid them to run. After that, the station ran commercials about their own programming, and the P.I. ads that made them the most money were mine and they ran them again and again and again.

Several national newscasters mentioned our ads, and Jay Leno commented on them during his opening monologues. As Roger Miller once said, "My face was on everybody's lips" and I was recognized wherever I went. But the greatest reward was the amount of folks lining up to buy tickets when we came back to Branson. Most of the theaters in Branson have to be extra friendly to bulk ticket buyers and cater to those who bring busses full of people. The bus buyers can deliver a vehicle with 40 or more people and for that they wanted a couple of free passes and deeply discounted tickets. They are powerful and some of them use their power with far less tact than others. You can't imagine how they reacted when all of their customers were expecting to see "The Ray Stevens Show" as part of their Branson tour and The Ray Stevens Theatre told them they were limiting their sale of bus tickets. Why give a three or four dollar discount for 40 people when you have long lines of people ready and willing to pay full price? I believe we were the only people in the history of Branson who limited bus ticket sales to a specific number per show.

During that second year in Branson, we brought in a video crew and taped the entire show so the next year, which was to be the last year of our three year run, we had another video for sale on TV. "Ray Stevens Live" covered one full hour of the main part of the Branson show and, as an up-sell, we offered "More Ray Stevens Live," which was the opening part of the show and featured the band, singer-comedian Janice Copeland, and fiddle player Nancy

Henson. The video with the up-sell sold another million copies and many more theatre tickets. We were selling out show after show but when the fall of 1993 came, my brain was fried and I was toast. Put a fork in me – I was done!

We sold the theatre for a significant down payment and carried the note on the remainder for the "Country Tonight" show, and it had a great run of almost ten years. I was glad they did so well and they paid their notes on time every month. Those years in Branson were a great run for me. Financially, it was the best years in my life, but it came at a cost. I had not been feeling well but I couldn't take time off and rest. I was tied to the whipping post, as they say. That theatre and all of those people who worked there were squarely on my back to carry. The stress of all that, along with a reaction from the steroid shots I was given to keep my voice from going out, had pushed me into diabetes. That was not a happy diagnosis, but it was not the worst news I was ever going to hear. But first, let me tell you a little bit about the other artists who performed in Branson.

CHAPTER 21

Branson Performers

There were (and are) a lot of great performers in Branson, and it was fun to be able to spend time with them while I was there.

Mel Tillis is a great singer and songwriter who has been voted Entertainer of the Year by the Country Music Association, and been in several movies. He wrote "Detroit City" for Bobby Bare and "Ruby Don't Take Your Love to Town" for Kenny Rogers. His career really started in 1957, when he wrote a song for Webb Pierce titled "I'm Tired." Melvin stutters, but I bet you knew that. He took what could have been a liability and turned it into a fabulous asset. I have known Mel for many years, both here in Nashville in the early days and in Branson later in our careers, where we both had successful theatre operations.

The stories about Mel are legendary. One of my favorites concerns him trying to hire a fiddle player. Mel loves fiddle players and the rumor is that he always thinks he can use one more, so he never met a fiddle player he didn't want to hire. There was a very hot fiddle player in town a while back, hot as a player and hot as concerns his popularity and visibility, which of course meant his price had gone up considerably, but Mel approached him about working with his band, The Statesiders. The fiddle player was interested but had some conditions. He would not ride on the bus with the rest of the band from gig to gig, but required Mel provide him a plane ticket for each show, First Class, and he needed his own dressing room and triple what Mel was paying his highest paid person on the road, per show. Mel thought a minute and reached in his pocket and handed the fiddle player his card and said "H-h-h-here Hoss. If you ever n-n-n-need a singer give me a c-c-call."

When Mel was younger, the story goes that he and a friend he called Fluffo partied long and hard without the benefit of the company of their wives. One night they came out of a club in Printer's Alley in downtown Nashville, each with a pretty young woman on their arm, and walked straight into their wives, who were coming into the same club. When someone asked Mel what they did, he replied in all seriousness "W-w-w-well I run and Fluffo f-f-f-faked a heart attack."

When Mel was in Branson, he made friends with another fiddle player who owns a very successful theatre and show. He is Shoji Tabuchi from Japan, who was helped along in his career by another fiddle player, Grand Ole Opry pioneer Roy Acuff. Shoji is a real All-American success story. He started out in Osaka, Japan, learned violin via the Suzuki method, got in to see Roy Acuff when a Grand Old Opry Show was touring Japan and, buoyed by Roy's encouragement, moved to the U.S.A. He played with several country bands from California to Kansas and finally in Nashville, where he did numerous appearances on the Grand Old Opry radio show as a guest of Mr. Acuff before deciding to take a gamble and open his own theatre in Branson. He hit the Jackpot! Shoji built an elaborate theatre in Branson and many people came to his show to see the ornate gold plated faucets and fixtures in the theatre restrooms as much as they did to see the show.

Mel and Shoji are friends and both love to fish in the many lakes around Branson. Mel told me one day that he had to quit fishing with Shoji because Shoji kept eating all of their bait.

I don't really mind Sushi myself, but it has to be heavily battered and deep southern fried.

Jim Stafford is a great songwriter, singer, and entertainer who found a home in Branson after a career in Los Angeles. He was once married to Bobbie Gentry of "Ode to Billy Joe" fame, and was a writer on the popular Smothers Brothers TV Show. Jim re-married a sweet gal from Texas named Anne, and they had two talented children later in his life who both appear in his show. On the subject of having kids late in life, Jim said that he and Anne were the only folks he knew who were looking for a retirement home in a good school district.

Jim was the first entertainer in Branson to work shows seven days a week. When I asked him why he would do such a thing – this was back before I opened the Ray Stevens Theatre – he said, "Think about it, what are you going to do with a night off in Branson?" At that time the nicest restaurant in town was the Dairy Queen, and he had a good point. Jim built a beautiful home on the Lake and a really nice theatre. It's a family business and Jim has had a wonderful run over there. He's a better man than I am to be able to do shows seven days a week. When I came to Branson, I did six days a week and spent the seventh day panting in an exhausted heap.

Mickey Gilley has a theatre and adjoining restaurant right on the Branson strip, across the street from Stafford's, and now does a TV show from there that runs on RFD-TV. Mickey had a bad fall at his condo not long ago, but I did his TV show the last time I was over there and I'm happy to say he's doing much better.

Moe Bandy is a fine singer and all around good fellow who has had a theatre in Branson for years. That's where

I met Mike Nichols. Mike is a talented singer and a performer who makes me laugh all the time. He says he is from Burnt Mattress, Arkansas, just a little above Hot Springs. He played a character in a TV Pilot I produced titled "We Ain't Dead Yet," about retired entertainers in a nursing home called The Encore. Mike's character is an old guy named Posterpedic. He says his father's name is Ortho and his mother's name is Temper.

Yakov Smirnoff is from Russia (imagine that!) and he has had a long and successful run in Branson. Like Jim Stafford, he came from Los Angeles where he had a recurring part on the popular comedy TV series "Night Court." He is from the province of Georgia that was part of the old Soviet Union, so when I released a video tape of his show on TV titled "What a Country," we formed a corporate entity and named it Georgia Boys. Yakov loves America and got his start working on cruise ships in the Baltic. He's one smart guy who took time to get a degree in Psychology while performing and managing his own theatre in Branson. Shoji and Yakov prove what a great country this really is.

Branson Encores

The Branson experience turned into a long goodbye. After selling the theatre at the end of the 1993 season, I went back on three different occasions.

My first return was in 1996 as a favor to a friend. Wayne Newton is known as one of the hardest working men in show business, and he is also a genuinely nice guy. He was booked in "The Wayne Newton Theatre" in Branson with a full schedule of shows, but a movie obligation came up during part of his performing season and he had a conflict. The movie was *Las Vegas Vacation*, which starred Chevy Chase in 1997. I had been away from Branson for three years, and it had taken me almost that long to recuperate. In Branson, you don't just roll in with your road show or casino show. They expect an opening act and full production. Well, I didn't have that much notice to put together a big production show, but I asked my daughter, Suzi, and her husband and co-writer Verlon Thompson, to handle the opening for me. It was a good opportunity for them and gave me a little breather. That only lasted six weeks while

Wayne filmed his part for the movie and then it was done. The next time I came back was in 2005. At the end of the 2003 season, the "Country Tonight" organization, who had faithfully paid their mortgage note every month for ten years, informed me that, due to the decline in their business in Branson, they were not able to make the last balloon payment. They asked if I would take back ownership of the theatre and allow them to continue making the same payments for another year as rent. I didn't particularly want to be in the theatre business again, but in the midst of those dark cloudy days there was a silver lining for me.

We took back the theatre, and between the 2003 and 2004 seasons I completely redecorated it. The theater needed it. During the time I was away it had become worn and ragged looking. We went in and reworked the seats, pulled out the carpet and put in new carpet. We repainted and replanted and reopened "The Ray Stevens Theatre," and "The Ray Stevens Show" came back one more time. Many of the same people who worked there earlier came back to work on stage and backstage again.

We wound up the old machine one more time, but it was not like the first run because Branson had changed significantly. When I first came to Branson, there were two major Nashville acts and a few who rotated in and out of the

Roy Clark Theatre. The rest were locals like the Presley family and Shoji Tabuchi. Now, the acts included Andy Williams, Tony Orlando, Bobby Vinton, Mel Tillis, Jim Stafford, Yakov Smirnoff, Moe Bandy, the Roy Rogers Museum and Theatre, Mickey Gilley, Wayne Newton, Glen Campbell, Charley Pride and others. The theatres offered morning shows, matinees, evening shows, kid shows and dinner shows. To put it mildly, the town had become over-built. We had a good two-year run and did good business, but it was nothing like the Gold Rush days of 1991-1993.

Still, we did great. I cut back the shows and times to make things more manageable, and we turned the theatre into an attractive money-making operation again. We had several people who wanted to buy it at the end of the second season in 2006, but I wanted to walk away without carrying a note for someone else this time. That's when someone contacted Patrick Gotch, the owner of RFD-TV, and let him know I was ready to sell.

RFD is a channel available in rural areas via satellite dish and on a few cable systems. They program to farmers, ranchers and equine people, and they wanted to purchase a theatre that was suitable for TV production. Ironically, when I designed my theatre, I did it with that in mind. There was a big pad where a production truck could park just off stage and I included large conduit tubes where power cables could be drawn into the off-stage area. It was made for TV production; in fact, the CBS Morning Show had broadcast from there and we produced a couple of videotaped performances. It was a natural.

RFD-TV bought the theatre in 2006, and I left the Branson experience behind me. At least, that's what I thought. In 2010, the management of the Welk Theatre and Resort made us an offer to come in for six weeks at the end of the summer, before the big Fall/Christmas season when they had a great show with Tony Orlando and the Lennon Sisters booked with lots of buses and buzz. They were going to be closed the whole year until we opened in mid-September and then close again at Christmas, after their Christmas show. That gives you an idea of how much Branson had changed in ten years. By this point, there were too many theaters, too many hotel rooms, too many no-name acts, too many discount ticket sellers, and too few Stars.

In 2009 I began doing my politically-oriented satirical material, and produced "internet videos" so I wanted to do two shows in Branson. Show number one would be "Patriots and Politics," and show number two would be "Such A Night – 50 Years of Hits and Hilarity," consisting of my hits down through the years. The people at the Welk Theater were concerned about how well the political material would go down, but I was sure that Branson was just as conservative as I was – so I had no worries. Hey, after all, this is America, freedom of speech and all that good stuff. Besides, we have a history in this country of folks like Mark Twain, Will Rogers, and other humorists who created names for themselves and made a pretty good living as political humorists.

Nevertheless, there was a little blow back. A couple of folks left a show or two and wanted their money back so we started paying attention and counting the complainers. Less than one percent of the people objected to my political material. That's over 99 percent approval rating. We had a CD/DVD combination of the political songs titled *We the People,* and we couldn't keep them in stock.

During the intermission at that first show, the concession stand was swamped with people wanting to buy that package. The theatre management was still concerned, so when Larry Welk, son of Lawrence Welk and the head of the entire Welk operation, was in town, he came to the show and told his staff afterwards that he thought the material was terrific and if anyone asked for their money back to give it to them. Further, if they were registered at the Welk hotel, they would be asked to leave. That was a ringing endorsement of the show as we continued to receive rave reviews from audiences. At the end of that run, we left Branson for what was probably the last time but, as Ian Fleming said in a famous James Bond book, "Never Say Never."

My good friend, Andy Williams, called and asked if I would be a part of his final season at the Moon River Theatre in 2012. He would open for me, I would do my show and he would come out at the end for us to do a couple of numbers together. How could I say no? So I excitedly signed up for a one-week run in October. But Andy passed away that summer of bladder cancer, and our duos were not to be. I did the shows as I had committed to my old friend who had been such a blessing to me and to my career. Rest in Peace, Andy.

CHAPTER 23

Pigeon Forge

There is another tourist area in addition to Branson that draws a lot of visitors – and it's a great place for entertainers, with several theatres and amusement parks as performance venues. It's closer to Nashville, right here in Tennessee, near Knoxville, in the eastern part of the State on the edge of the Smokey Mountain National Park and Gatlinburg.

I have played Pigeon Forge numerous times over the years doing one nighters, but I have also been attracted to it as a possible place to build a theatre. Before I made the decision to go to Branson, I looked that situation over carefully because another entertainer opened a theme park there back in 1986. Dolly Parton's Dollywood has been a fabulous success. At some point along the line, and I'm not aware of just when, Dolly and Dollywood got into business with the Herschend brothers, Jack and Pete, who own the theme park, Silver Dollar City, in Branson. They also operate the Stone Mountain Park just outside my old home town of Atlanta and they, along with Dolly, co-own the Dixie Stampede attractions.

The Herschend brothers owned a theme park or attraction of some kind in Pigeon Forge since the late 1970s. Lee Greenwood had a theatre there and so did my old friend, Louise Mandrell, with whom I had worked the Desert Inn in Las Vegas. Lots of Nashville acts like T.G. Shepherd and others have successfully worked there for years.

It had become obvious to HFE (Herschend Family Entertainment, the Herschend family business entity) that the idea of tagging a theme park with a celebrity name in an area that attracts southern families and country music fans was a real winner. During that time my career was rolling along very well on the strength of songs like "It's Me Again Margaret," "Would Jesus Wear a Rolex on His Television Show," and "Mississippi Squirrel Revival." All were on MCA Records, who had released the double album set of *Get the Best of Ray Stevens* via TV commercials that were playing everywhere.

One day I got a call. Jack and Pete Herschend wanted to fly over from Branson in their corporate plane to talk to me about something. Of course I said yes. I was curious and it never hurts to talk, or at least listen. Jack Herschend is the older of the two and is a power house of a personality, a country boy that you don't want to under-estimate. I understand that he was a whiz of a vacuum cleaner salesman in his youth, and after his Daddy's death he took over a Cave attraction the family owned in Missouri. He and his brother, Pete, eventually turned that into Silver Dollar City. They drew lots of people when they lighted the cave and put in a motorized tour and gave silver dollars in change. They constantly added to the attraction and did great Fall business each year with a crafts festival, etc.

When the "Beverly Hillbillies" TV show on CBS was popular, the producer, Paul Henning, who was also from the Missouri Ozarks, shot some episodes there, which really put Silver Dollar City and Branson on the map.

Jack and Pete wanted to talk to me about a theme park that I would lend my name to and where I would perform a few dates each year. There would be fun family rides called "Don't Look Ethel" and the "Mississippi Squirrel Rollercoaster" with an "Everything is Beautiful" theme that fit with their sincere Christian values. I was flattered to say the least, and they made me a generous offer of a guaranteed $1 million a year for the use of my name. They also wanted to book me a certain number of dates at the venue at a generous per show price. I don't remember now whether the offer was for a theme park in Pigeon Forge, or Branson, or both.

To tell the truth, I don't know why I didn't jump at the offer of a "Ray Stevens Fun Land" no matter where it was, but I must have had my mind focused on something else. Like when Burt Bacharach offered "Raindrops Keep Falling on My Head" and I turned it down because I was focused on the recording I had just made of "Sunday Morning Comin' Down." I don't know what I was thinking, but I passed.

I don't spend a lot of time looking back, but "looking back" maybe I should have taken their offer. I didn't completely forget about it or ignore the fact that some very astute businessmen were willing to sink a large chunk of money into a venture that depended on my name drawing large crowds. The memory of that meeting was in my mind when Jim Thomas, who owned the Roy Clark Theatre in Branson, offered me the chance to perform an entire season of shows there in 1991. Yeah, Branson was calling my name loud and clear back then and I'm sure I made the right choice by opening my own theatre there instead of Nashville or Pigeon Forge. But, hey, I just might do something like that yet, because retirement just has no appeal for me at all.

CHAPTER 24

I'm Not Dead Yet

I slipped and fell on the icy front steps of my office back in the 1970s and broke my jaw. I had it wired shut for two weeks and lived on chocolate shakes and canned chili that I sucked through a big straw after it was liquefied in a blender. Then, while driving back from Kentucky one rainy night, my car wheel wells became clogged with mud and my brother John, who was in the back seat, and my manager Don Williams, who was in the front passenger seat, and I went end-over-end and finally slid downhill upside down, with the rear window glass out and the car acting like a scoop. When we finally stopped, John emerged from the back seat covered with mud and held out his wrist with his Timex watch and declared "It's still ticking!" Later, there was a wrestler named Ray Stevens who passed away unexpectedly a few years ago and ever since his demise I have had to correct folks who were convinced I was the Ray Stevens who died. After correcting them, most folks accept the fact that I am still alive and it's actually me talking to them. I've had some close calls but there was another event that caused people to really wonder about my health or lack thereof.

The run in Branson was difficult physically, but very successful financially, as both a theatre operation and a springboard for promoting my videos. Over 1.6 million people saw the show and they spread the news to all their family and friends. The 3.2 million people who bought the *Comedy Video Classics* and *Ray Stevens LIVE* did the same. My name recognition level was as high as it had ever been in my career, but I was as tired as I had ever been. The stress of the shows and the schedule of several performances a day, six days a week, along with the injections that medical doctors gave me during that three-year period to keep my throat from shutting down and my voice from disappearing, had caused me to test positive for diabetes. It was a bummer, but I was glad to hear the reason I felt so bad so I could clear the way to correct the problem. You tell me how to fix something that's broken and I'll do it. When the doctor told me "You're diabetic, don't eat sugar" I stopped eating sugar immediately and immediately began to feel better.

Like I said earlier, the diabetes diagnosis was not the worst news I was ever to receive. I had begun to get the hang of this no sugar deal when I went to the doctor for my annual check-up and received a call a few days later that said "No need for concern but I think we need to do some more tests because your PSA levels are a little elevated." You probably already know this, but for those who don't, PSA stands for Prostate Specific Antigen. When there is a possibility of cancer in the prostate, this PSA level increases; however, there are false positives and negatives in the initial test so doctors view it as an indication that a closer look is required. After more tests and that closer look, I got another call, telling me "No need for concern but because of that last test we think a biopsy would be wise." So I got the biopsy and this time the call said "No need for concern, but you have prostate cancer. We can cut it out and you'll be fine."

NO NEED FOR CONCERN?!!? I didn't hear anything after the voice said CANCER. It's the worst thing you ever want a doctor to tell you and the most asinine thing they can say before they tell you there is NO NEED FOR CONCERN!

I began checking out my options and there were a few. One was "Watchful Waiting," which means you do nothing but watch and wait to see what happens. This is only an option for the elderly because prostate cancer is usually slow-growing, so you watch and wait to see if you don't die of something else before the cancer gets you. I was too young and too concerned by the diagnosis to watch and especially wait. I'm not good at waiting, even for a traffic light. I wanted to do something. It was like that old cartoon with two starving buzzards sitting on a limb and one turns to the other and says "Patience Hell! I'm gonna kill something!" I'm not going to sit around and wait when I've discovered that something lethal is growing inside of me. Something's wrong. Let's fix it.

A second option was "General Radiation." With this option, the entire region of your groin is blasted with radiation treatments in order to kill the prostate cancer. If it works, the final result is a good thing, but along the way the radiation kills most everything else down there as well. I understood it to be a long, drawn-out painful process, that leaves you with a critical area of your body that does not function well. I did not plan to have more children, but I had not planned on giving up the activity that produced them just yet. The idea of reduced bladder control didn't sound like something I wanted to deal with either, especially during a time I was on stage in front of a few thousand people.

I seriously considered the third option. It was also a radiation treatment, but was not a blast to the entire region. This option involved the implantation of radioactive seeds directly into the prostate gland in the specific area where the cancer has been detected. The side effects included some of the same problems as the other radiation, but reports indicated that it was more controlled. I liked that option, so I was leaning in that direction.

The fourth option was surgery, which had been recommended to me as the one sure-fire, life-saving, no doubt best chance of beating any spread of cancer once and for all. The surgeon goes in, snips the prostate on one end and then the other end and connects the conduit on either side and you go home cancer-free. You also go home with the strong possibility of a leaky bladder and the definite cessation of all sexual activity forevermore.

I favored the radiation seeds option because it limited the downside problems in the treatment. It didn't guarantee a perfect outcome, but at least it offered a good chance. Before I gave the O.K. for that, my long-time friend Buddy Kalb called Dr. Lee Brock, a friend who was a surgeon in Kansas City. Dr. Brock told Buddy that he had undergone prostate cancer surgery at Johns Hopkins Hospital in Baltimore. A surgeon there, Dr. Patrick Walsh, was pioneering a new "nerve-sparing" surgery. It seemed like every physician who had prostate cancer wanted to have this surgery done by Dr. Walsh, but it was quite difficult if not impossible to get to him. Dr. Walsh had written a book, *The Prostate: A Guide for Men and the Women Who Love Them*" which Buddy read. He told me about this book and encouraged me to read it as well. Buddy thought this treatment was the way to go and told me that if I read the book and agreed, he would make an appointment for me to see Dr. Walsh.

Dr. Patrick Walsh had been a pediatric surgeon who was skillful in dealing with tiny blood vessels in infants. For his pioneering prostate surgery technique, he meticulously extracted the nerves around a prostate gland before taking it out of the body, leaving the nerves necessary for bladder control and sexual function in place rather than cutting them out with the prostate. It was a time consuming procedure for the surgeon, but it had a proven history of producing not only an escape from cancer, but the retention of quality-of-life functions. I was all for it, so Buddy went to work making calls and I don't know how he managed it, but in a few days we were on a plane headed for Baltimore. At Johns Hopkins, we met with Dr. Walsh, who examined me and reviewed my files, reports, and tests. He then looked me in the eye and said, "I am going to operate on you, remove the cancer from your body and you will be fine." I fully believed him and signed up immediately.

Dr. Walsh was right. He performed the surgery, I recovered on schedule, and I am now fine and have been ever since the day of that operation. To all the men reading this book – or listening to a wife reading this book – I've got some good advice for you – make sure you get a regular physical exam and insist on a PSA test. If it comes up positive, read the book by Dr. Patrick Walsh and do whatever you think is best. You know what I think is best and that I'm glad I made the decision that I made. Dr. Patrick Walsh has trained surgeons all around the world in his technique, so it is now probable that a surgeon trained by him is available at a hospital near you who can perform his nerve-sparing prostate surgery.

Later, I recorded a song about my experiences called "The PSA Song" and the lyrics tell the whole story and closes with an encouragement for all men over 50 to get a PSA test. Since that's the way the song ends, and is such very good advice, that's how I'll end this chapter.

CHAPTER 25

An Encyclopedia of Recorded Comedy Music

I guess it's no surprise that one of the loves of my life is Comedy Music. In many ways I am a walking encyclopedia of recorded comedy music. From the time I was a little kid, I have been attracted to songs on the radio that made me smile or laugh out loud. Those songs were a part of the fabric of my All-American life growing up, but things change and music is no exception.

I don't understand the appeal of some contemporary music, so I have become like my parents, I guess. I would like to preserve something of the golden age of Comedy/Novelty songs, and as one the Last Men Standing in that field, I believe I am uniquely qualified to do so. That thought led me to launch an ambitious project to faithfully re-record the most popular comedy songs of all-time using the latest recording technology. I wanted to include the most popular songs in the comedy genre since I first became aware of them, up until today. I had to put a limit on the number of songs so I decided to choose one hundred songs that, in my opinion, would best represent the comedy genre to the next generation.

I went back to the 1940s, my earliest memories, and covered each of the following decades up to the current time. I'll probably have to do an amended follow-up edition, but I'm pretty happy with what I included in *Ray Stevens Encyclopedia of Recorded Comedy Music*. It is a one hundred and eight song boxed set package (OK so I ran a little over) with extensive encyclopedic notes on the artists, writers and the impact the songs had during their era. It was released in 2012. It took two years of my life in the studio recording and mixing, and a lifetime of collecting the songs and the memories. I'm proud of it and my only regret is I keep remembering songs I wish I had included. Still, I believe I was able to pull together a sizable representative sample of a fading genre.

As I write this I am working on another project, *Melancholy Fescue,* which will be an album of songs done bluegrass style that were not originally written in that style. Songs like "Misty" and "You Are So Beautiful" are good examples, but this time I'm working on arrangements with a symphony in mind so this is High-Class Bluegrass. I'm also working on an album that I call *Nouveaux Retro,* which consists of famous old songs done in a brand new way.

I'm finishing up a double gospel album I've been working on and I'm also excited about a musical, *Seeds*, about Johnny Appleseed, that I hope to see on stage soon. There is another musical production written by Buddy titled *A Mississippi Squirrel Revival*. That's a two act musical featuring the Squirrel song and about 15 others, all set in a fairly typical small southern town church service. We premiered and taped the performance recently and it was an out-of-the-park Home Run. I hope you see it when it is performed near you.

But that's not all. I have two movie scripts that were written for me by Billy Field that are exciting. Both are family films with one about that Mississippi Squirrel, and another about playing the game of marbles called "Playing for Keeps."

Beyond all this who knows? No doubt something will strike me funny or touch me in a way that I'll feel compelled to write and/or sing about it. Sometimes a talented writer in Nashville will bring me a song that I feel I just have to do. We will find ways to get it in front of the public and give them a chance to hear it and own a copy. That's what the music business is about and what it has always been about, from the days when sheet music and piano rolls were sold, up through the days of cylinders, then vinyl records, cassettes, 8-tracks, CDs or, now, downloads.

How people obtain their music changes, but what is constant is that writers write, musicians play, singers sing, and people want to listen. It's the delivery system that changes, so we have to be flexible and forward thinking. Along with sensing what the public wants to hear, we have to anticipate new ways of presenting it and we need to figure out how to make money marketing it so we can keep on doing it.

I can't wait until tomorrow. Nashville and Music City is as exciting today as it was when I first came here as a kid to make my first recording for Prep records. Back then we only had three or four tracks to record on, and now every instrument, every voice, every drum or cymbal can have its own track. Every possible kind of nuanced sound is available. Effects are at your finger tips with the push of a button. The old methods of splicing, patching and pinging are visually represented on a computer screen now and done instantly. If the singer can't stay in key, there's a button for that. It's an exciting world and I'm happy to still be a part of it.

If I had another multi-million selling hit today, what would I do with the money? The same as I'd do if I won the Lottery. As I said earlier, I would just keep recording as long as I am able to play, sing, write, and record – until I'd spent it all, I guess.

I'm no longer just a musician. In addition to the publishing business and several pieces of real estate on Music Row and around town that I rent out for office space, I own a video production studio and three recording studios in my complex at the corner of 17th and Grand Avenue. I also have a video editing suite and keep current with what's going on out there on the web.

It's a full time job for someone to manage the commercial real estate but in addition to my primary residence, I own a small house in a modest neighborhood near the Green Hills section in Nashville that I've had for years. I just can't seem to bring myself to part with that house, as well as a beach house in Gulf Shores, Alabama. The beach house has given me lots of opportunities to express that "beaver" nature since it's been hit by two hurricanes. It was once built and owned by the governor of Alabama, and was truly well-built.

I like going to Gulf Shores but don't get down there very often. I have friends there. Phil Everly of the Everly Brothers has a place close to mine, and so does Harry Warner. Harry worked as Writer Relations Manager for Broadcast Music Inc. for years and has been a good friend to me since I don't know when. He was a friend of Bill Lowery and a friend of Felton Jarvis. Felton helped Harry get into the music business. Harry worked for Jerry

Reed for several years as well as BMI, and was also a close friend of Chet Atkins – so our little network in Nashville has been very close and pretty small.

I like the music business. I like publishing, and I enjoy real estate. People ask me why I don't take vacations. When you enjoy what you do every day, why take a day off? I think vacations are mostly made for people who can't stand their jobs and need a few days or weeks every year to go somewhere and do what they really enjoy. I really enjoy what I do every day. Besides, Nashville is my home and when I'm gone I can hardly wait to get back. With the exception of those days spent traveling all over the world to sing my songs, I've spent most of my time in Davidson County, Tennessee.

I have numerous Gold Records and BMI and ASCAP performance awards hanging on the walls, and I hope I've made a positive contribution to the growth and development of this city where I have lived for over fifty years.

Nashville has been very good to me and for me, and I only hope that I've been good to and for Nashville. But sometimes it's hard to get the acceptance you would like to have in your own hometown.

CHAPTER 26

A Piano Man in a Guitar Town

Truckers have a lingo all their own. On their C.B.'s they call Atlanta "The Big A," Casper, Wyoming, is "Ghost City," and Nashville is "Guitar Town." That's Nashville's reputation, and almost everyone who comes here following a dream is carrying a guitar case. But I'm a piano man. My first band, The Barons, didn't have a guitar player in it, and my signature hit, "Everything is Beautiful," did not have a guitar on the session. In many ways that is a picture of my life here: A Piano Man in a Guitar Town, A Pop Singer in the Country Music Capitol of the world.

Being a piano man was an asset in the beginning because guitar players waiting to become session players or recording artists were in a line that stretched out the door, down the block and half way back to Alabama.But keyboard players were fairly few. My pal, Jerry Reed, did well as a guitar player when he came to town because of his enormous talent, unique style, and the fact that THE Guitar Player of all Guitar Players, Chet Atkins, recognized Jerry's talent and gave him his Blue Ribbon Seal of Approval. Almost every guitar picker in the world admired Chet Atkins' mastery of the guitar, and Chet admired Reed and a few others. Chet created a little elite fraternity that included John Knowles, Steve Wariner, Tommy Emmanuel, and Jerry Reed. He called them "C.G.P.'s" for "Certified Guitar Pickers" – the Best of the Best.

It's true that most acts in town pick a guitar and many of them wear cowboy boots and/or a cowboy hat and are comfortable sitting with just their guitar and entertaining folks with their songs like the cowboys around a campfire in the movies. I don't know how Nashville, in the middle of Tennessee, got tagged with the cowboy image. Eddy Arnold called himself the Tennessee Plowboy, and there are a lot more Plowboys than Cowboys in this town. "Country and Western" is the old label for most of the music made in Nashville, but the music is more accurately "Country and Southern!!"

Folks will often call on an artist to do an acoustic set, an unplugged performance, and it's easy for them because that's how they started. It's kind of relaxed and charming with just the singer and an acoustic guitar. That doesn't work for me and, while I'm southern to the core, I don't fit the Cowboy or the Plowboy image and never have. Donny and Marie Osmond had a hit, "A Little Bit Country and A Little Bit Rock and Roll," but when I came to town I was "Very Little Country and a Whole Lot of Rhythm and Blues." So was Ronnie Milsap. He and Jerry Lee Lewis, along with Charlie Rich, were Rock and Roll and Rhythm and Blues piano pickers and singers who made the switch to country songs that fit comfortably on the country charts. But not me.

The people who compile the charts in the trade magazines have never known what to do with me and my music. I didn't grow up listening to just one kind of music. I have always liked all kinds of music and I have played Rhythm and Blues piano on a country song, and country piano on a pop song. I'm not stuck in any one particular groove. Actually, there's not a lot of difference between a groove and a rut.

I have never thought of Nashville as Country Music City. To me, it's Music City U.S.A. Once I was appearing on the Grand Ole Opry, broadcast from the stage of the Ryman Auditorium – the Mother Church of Country Music as they say – and as we did the sound check before the show I said, "I need a little more saxophone in my monitor," whereupon Larry Gatlin commented, "Now there's something you don't often hear on this stage."

Being versatile has had its ups and downs, but it opened

a lot of doors for me as a session player. I've played organ, piano, and trumpet, and sung background on other artist's sessions, and regularly play bass, drums, keyboards, horns, and sing most of the background parts on my own records. But being an outsider is never fun, and I think that's how many in the traditional Nashville country music community see me. Like those who compile the charts; they don't know where to put me or how to type-cast me.

I know I haven't helped them because I keep doing different things. About the time I get classified as a pop act, I'll do a comedy song and then, when folks are sure I'm a comedy act, I'll do a country ballad. I haven't been much help to people who like to classify me, but I like doing what interests me, not whatever fits somebody else's idea of me.

I'm not exclusively a comedy performer or a pop vocalist or a country singer, although I have been given numerous accolades and awards and my recordings have reached the top of a number of various charts to validate any of those classifications. Mainly, I'm a musician; specifically, a Nashville musician. If you're a Nashville studio musician, you have to be able to play anything with an appreciation for the music you are making, whether it is rock, pop, gospel, country, or whatever. I've worked with R&B acts such as Lloyd Price and Clyde McPhatter, opened for the great Las Vegas comedian Shecky Greene, and played on sessions with numerous acts in numerous styles, from Elvis to Dolly Parton.

In addition to being a Nashville musician, I am an old-school entertainer. The traditional country singer with a single hit goes on stage and says "Howdy," plays cover songs for 30 minutes, finishes with his hit, says "Thank You, Folks," walks off stage, onto a bus and heads for the next town. Others, who have a string of hits, shoot off fireworks, swing on ropes, hang from the rafters and bust guitars while they sing their hits for an hour or two and then take a limo to their Gulf-Stream Jet and fly to the next town while their fleet of buses and semis follow.

I don't have a bus or a Gulf-Stream Jet, and I don't like limos. I like being close enough to the folks to have fun with them for an hour or so. I love to play my piano and sing my little songs. My idea of entertainment is sharing laughs and good music and have folks go away feeling lighter and better than they did when they came in. I don't care if anyone labels me country or pop or anything else. I just want to be known as a person whose music they appreciate and whose jokes their whole family can enjoy. I want them to leave entertained.

The Powers That Be in Nashville, whoever "they" are, often have problems with singers who don't conform to their idea of a Nashville artist. The most recent example is

Taylor Swift. Folks say she's not really country, and then go on to say she can't really sing, to which I reply, "She can sing plenty well enough and she can really write and communicate with her audience."

That young lady knows her audience and knows how to deliver what they want. She deserves tremendous respect for what she has accomplished and how she conducts herself as she does it. All of Nashville should embrace her, but some complain she's not Country. Many of those same folks did not want to listen to or work with me when I attempted to help make the Music Theatre business that was booming in Branson happen in Nashville. That meant that I had to go to Branson and build my theatre there. All during that time people asked, "Have you moved to Branson? Have you left Nashville?"

When I had the biggest record of the year of any genre with "The Streak," the Country Music Association ignored that achievement. Nashville left me on a couple of occasions, but I have never left Nashville. This is my home. No matter where I go, "my heart keeps going back to Nashville," as I wrote in my song. It may be known as Guitar Town, Hillbilly Hollywood, or Country Music City, but I love it. Nashville has been the place for me. There are great pickers and great recording centers elsewhere, but I would never have been able to tolerate the traffic of Los Angeles, the congestion of New York, the heat of Miami, or the small size of Muscle Shoals. As a Nashville Cat, which is another name for a Nashville session player, I recorded in all of those places but was still able to live in the Southern comfort zone that is uniquely Nashville, Tennessee.

The "Powers That Be" may have overlooked me from time to time, but the regular friendly folks of Nashville have embraced me and made me feel right at home, even though I'm no more country than Taylor Swift and I don't really play guitar, as anyone who has ever seen me perform "Gitarzan" can attest.

Nashville cannot be pigeon-holed as just one thing, regardless of the way some people like to think. It's not just Guitar Town. Nashville has a major society event every year called the Swan Ball. It's a big-time black tie, champagne and caviar event that is the highlight of the social season. During that same time, a bunch of Good Ol' Boys put on the Swine Ball. It's a beer and barbeque, dress in overalls with shoes optional event. Over the years, I have received invitations to both of those diverse functions by friends who are prominent in each group. I'm right proud of that.

CHAPTER 27

Name Dropping

It occurred to me as I was writing this book that there are a lot of people who have been very important to me in my life that I may not have mentioned due to the way I chose to tell my story. This book is not about my entire life or about everyone who has ever been a part of my life, but there are a lot of people who should not go unmentioned if I am going to write anything about my life. It would be just plain wrong not to name some of the people I have known who played a significant part in my life and career. Since there will most likely never be another chance for me to do this, I will include a partial list of those people in this chapter.

Most of my childhood days in Clarkdale, Georgia, were spent with two guys, Larry Gilbert and Kay Moon. We enjoyed long summers together playing and swimming at the community pool. They were a big part of my childhood. In Albany, where I spent all but my last year of high school, there were two beautiful girls: Barbara Able and Lynn Ventulett.

In Atlanta, in addition to the folks already mentioned at Druid Hills High School and at Bill Lowery's N.R.C. Record Company and Recording Studio, there were several people who helped me along my way. One was Cotton Carrier, a local country singer on TV who became a song-plugger for Bill Lowery's music publishing companies. Cotton and Mary Talent, who was Bill's secretary, were the backbone of Lowery's Atlanta office. Joe South, Tommy Roe, Ric Cartey, Mac Davis, Billy Joe Royal, Paul Peek, and the Tams were all recording artists there while Butch, Cherri, and Terri Lowery were Bill's kids who grew up working in the music business.

Priscilla Mitchell was a great singer who did a lot of background vocal work and became Prissy Hubbard when she married Jerry Hubbard, who became Jerry Reed. There were D.J.s in and around Atlanta like Paul Drew, Bob McKee, and Ray Kenneman who were helpful to me, as well as musicians who were fun to know like Jimmy Estes, Ray Jones, Nelson Rogers, and Jeff Richards. I especially remember Jeff because he always wore cool shoes. He went to Hollywood to work in TV westerns. Sheb Wooley, who wrote and recorded "The Flying Purple People-Eater," had done the same thing with great success several years before. Sheb was a bad guy in the movie *High Noon,* the principal in the film *Hoosiers* and starred in the TV series

"Rawhide" and also worked in lots of Hollywood westerns. Sheb was Roger Miller's neighbor in Oklahoma where they both grew up. What a small world we live in.

In Nashville, I have worked with the best musicians in town over the past 50 years and want to shine a spotlight on some who have been important to me and my career. Steve Gibson is a great musician and is now Music Director for the Grand Ole Opry; I've worked with Steve for years. Steve, Jerry Kroon, Roger Morris, Randy Cullers, and Stuart Keathly worked the road with me for a number of years. Jim Stephany was my road manager for quite a while; Jim is a long-time friend of Bobby Goldsboro, who is also a good friend and who is one funny guy to hang with. Raymond Hicks, who worked for the Oak Ridge Boys for years, became my road manager after Jim left. Raymond married the talented Deborah Allen and now manages her career.

Gary Prim is a great keyboard session player, and Tommy Wells and Scott Weckerly are great drummers who you can hear on many of my records. Sadly, Tommy passed away recently. That's happening too often these days. My most recent band members are Dennis Solee, Larry McCoy, John Hamrick, and Fred Newell. Fred and Larry Sasser spent several years on "Nashville Now" with Ralph Emery's band conducted by Jerry Whitehurst. Larry

Sasser was my steel guitar player for years while Lisa Silver played fiddle and sang background vocals. Lisa leads a background vocal group that I use on many sessions and she is the Cantor at the local Jewish Temple. Jerry Kimbrough and John Clausey are two other great and talented guitar pickers who have worked with me.

I sometimes play the Opry or participate in one of the various awards shows and, as I said before, it's fun to renew old friendships and associations backstage. I recently visited with Steve Wariner and Ricky Skaggs, two great musicians. I enjoyed that visit, but it made me realize how many friends I have lost in the not-so-distant past, like George "Goober" Lindsay, Grandpa Jones, Minnie Pearl, Chet Atkins, Gordon Stoker of the Jordanaires, George Jones, and Owen Bradley.

I have been fortunate to work with some really great musician/producers in Nashville, such as Jerry Crutchfield, who produced Tanya Tucker. Tanya once gave me a puppy while we were playing in Las Vegas. What do you do when someone gives you a puppy and you're out of town? I just said "Thank You," and took him home with me. Penny and I named him L.V. (the initials stand for either Las Vegas or Ludwig Von as in Beethoven, take your pick – and we loved him every day of his playful life.)

Norro Wilson produced Charley Pride, Tammy Wynette,

Eddy Arnold, John Anderson, and many others before he teamed with Buddy Cannon, a former member of Mel Tillis's band, to produce Kenny Chesney. Buddy is still producing, but Norro and Purvis have retired. You may want to ask who is Purvis – but it's better if you don't.

Other great producers I've worked with were Jerry Kennedy, Ron Chancey, and Bob Montgomery.

I've also worked with some incredibly fine studio engineers like Charlie Tallent, and my current right-hand man, Ben Surratt. Ben was recommended to me by Clark Hagen, another engineer who was introduced to me by Chet and left to move to Denver. I've been fortunate to make some really good records with the help of those three talented men.

There were a lot of acts who worked in Branson who I have known and admired for years that I've already mentioned. Then there was Glen Campbell, who had a nice run in Branson. One afternoon I sat backstage, struggling to fasten a camel leg around my own so I could "ride out" on stage in my Clyde the Camel prop. Glen walked up to me, looked at my prop and said "Well, it's come to this has it?"

For a while it seemed like everyone was headed to Branson to perform. People like Bobby Vinton and Tony Orlando from my early Rock n'Roll tour days were there. Tony had Toni Wine from New York with him to play keyboards and sing in his show. Toni Wine has perfect pitch and is a lot of fun. I remember that Mike Shepherd and I once dropped by a studio in New York where she was recording and she had us clap hands on the record. The song was "Sugar Sugar" and it was a big hit. I have always felt that it was our superb hand clapping that made that record a hit.

Linda Kay Lance, who was once a recording act in Nashville, helped my brother John in the gift shop at the Ray Stevens Theatre. She did a great job, and so did Lee Caruthers with the food concessions. During our last run in Branson, Dick Gossum, a friend and flying buddy of John's, came over to help and he met and married Lee. There were so many wonderful people in Branson and I wish I could remember and name them all. I do remember that Dee Murphy and her husband Wayne, an ex- Missouri Highway Patrolman, were a great help.

Janice Copeland is a great singer and comedienne who played Jane in my "Gitarzan" production and the opera singer Bev in "The Streak." She performed in a Nordic helmet, horns and all. Janice and Nancy Henson, a red-headed fiddle player who had been playing fiddle since she was three, were great assets to our Branson shows. Both came to Nashville to work with me in a series of shows at the Acuff Theatre at Opryland during the Christmas Season.

I produced a TV pilot titled "We Ain't Dead Yet," and worked with a wonderful production crew headed by Randy Hale and his ever-present assistant, Fabianna. That cast included many of the folks already mentioned, but I want to recognize Kevin King, a talented guy who was in the show as a State Inspector. I was also joined by Louise Mandrell, with whom I worked the Desert Inn in Las Vegas a few times, and my friend Phil Everly of the Everly Brothers duo. Last but by no means least is the very funny Mike Nichols. I met Mike while he was working with Moe Bandy, another great singer in Branson. Mike's humor still breaks me up.

Don Murry Grubbs is a very talented young publicity agent who has helped me in recent years. I marvel at how mature and together he is. When I was his age, I was clueless about the things he is so comfortable with and capable of doing.

Don got me booked on the Mike Huckabee show a couple of times and I really enjoyed meeting the Governor. He's a real renaissance man; Baptist Minister, Arkansas State Governor, Bass player, National Talk Show Host, and all around good guy. If things don't go well for me, maybe I can hold cue cards for him on his TV show or help take up the offering if he goes back to preaching. If things don't work out for him, he can play Bass in my band. Southern boys can survive, as the talented Hank Jr. has said, but we have to look out for one another.

Another person who has been a good friend through the years is Larry Black, who has recently had outstanding success on TV with his down home "Larry's Diner" show on RFD-TV. Larry and his crew know how to make you feel special.

I hate to think that I've left out some important names, but I probably have. Well, that's the way it goes. As one of my favorite prayers from a kid's prayer book goes, "Dear God, I'm doing the best I can. Love Ray."

Writing this book has caused me to take a good, long look back down the stairway of success that I have climbed in the music business – and the steps are pretty clear to me now. The first big step was Bill Lowery, but he was much more than a step; he was a NASA launching pad. He provided the enthusiasm that fueled my dreams and, more than that, he provided a priceless education. Bill's Record Company, NRC, or National Recording Company, and his recording studio in Atlanta allowed me an unbelievable opportunity to learn daily all of the basics of studio recording and to experiment. I produced, arranged vocal parts, and guided the musicians as we made recording after recording for Bill, who was relentless in his search for hits. I was allowed to mix the music and voices after the sessions were completed, and go in and sweeten different parts of the record with strings after I lived with the basic tracks for a while. There was no clock for me. I had unlimited access to all of the "toys." Most importantly, I had Bill's trust, encouragement, and confidence. During those first few years, while my folks were happy that I was attending college at Georgia State preparing myself for a "real job," I acquired the equivalent of a Doctorate in Rock'n'Roll Top 40 Music Production. It was at Lowery Music, Bill's music publishing company, where I learned about publishing, which prepared me for ownership of my own four music publishing companies.

I don't know where a young person could go today to get that kind of education. Bill had a recording studio, a pressing plant, a promotion department, and music publishing company all at one location. He added an important ingredient, Success, that made it all profitable. There is a Christian University here on Music Row, Belmont, that started a Music Business curriculum years ago in an effort to help people get started in the music business and acquire a resume that prepares them for a career in the music industry. Mike Curb has made a great donation of time and money to help those programs. However, although it is well intentioned, that program can only scratch the surface of what I learned in Atlanta with

Bill. I admire Belmont and they have graduated people who have made important contributions to the business, but there are some things that just can't be taught in a classroom. The only way to learn them is for someone to make mistakes and discoveries as they work each day in the world of the music business. I cherish the education I received at NRC under Professor Lowery who, instead of trying to teach me anything with lectures, set me free like a kid in a candy store and allowed me to learn. That experience was priceless, and that first step made all of the other steps possible. Like step number two: Ken Nelson.

Ken Nelson was the head of Capitol Records' Nashville division and he was the one who, at the urging of Bill, listened to my record of "Silver Bracelet" and decided to release it on Prep, a new subsidiary of Capitol. But Ken did much more than that. He took the recording Bill produced, re-recorded and re-mixed it and made it a far better record. Bill was a lot of wonderful things, but he was not a record mixer, at least not at that time.

Ken was an important step for another reason; he changed me from Ray Ragsdale into Ray Stevens. I wasn't sure how important that really was early in my career, but I have become comfortable being Ray Stevens. It goes beyond Ray Stevens being a better name for a career in show business; it also helped a young kid see himself differently, with greater potential and possibilities. Whatever the reason, it was Ken Nelson who made my first regional hit possible on a national label and introduced Ray Stevens to a wide audience. That made step number three possible: Shelby Singleton.

Shelby Singleton was the Mercury Records executive who ran their Nashville office in the late 1950s and early 1960s. On the strength of the popularity of "Silver Bracelet," made popular by the disc jockeys in the Southeast and Atlanta area who played my record on the radio, I got to work on the "Georgia Jubilee" show in East Point, Georgia. Shelby brought J.P. Richardson, "The Big Bopper," to the "Georgia Jubilee" one Saturday to promote his new single, "Chantilly Lace," and we met. Shelby was a friend of Bill Lowery, and later offered me a job. While he wanted to have me make records for Mercury, he also needed someone to help him get the Mercury operation in Nashville up and running. Shelby knew what I had done in and around Lowery's studio and, through Bill's blessing, offered me a job in Nashville.

Bill could have tried to block me leaving him, but he wanted what was best for me. How many people have angels like that on their stairway? It was Shelby Singleton who gave me a chance to bat in the big league on a regular basis. Bill Lowery and Ken Nelson gave me my initial exposure to the music business and the folks who made it hum, but Shelby made me a player in the starting rotation. This put me in the position to come to the attention of Fred Foster.

Fred Foster gave me the opportunity to further educate myself about the music business and to work with some of my heroes. Nashville was pretty much Country Music City during the time that Fred moved to town from the Washington/Baltimore area and acquired acts from Memphis like Roy Orbison. Fred had a decidedly pop slant on music. At Monument, I met my life-long friend, Mike Shepherd, and had the hit "Gitarzan." Fred gave me the opportunity to work with Boots Randolph and learn arranging at the side of Bill Justis, who gave me the title to the song "Gitarzan." During my time with Fred, Roger Miller introduced me to a man who became my manager for 25 years, Don Williams. Don, and his brother, Andy Williams, were my next big step.

Andy Williams had one of the most successful TV shows in the country when I appeared on it several times. Andy offered me the opportunity to host his summer replacement show, which ran on the NBC network during a prime time slot for eight weeks. What an opportunity! What exposure! After that show, Ray Stevens was a nationally known name. Before then, I was only known to fans who heard me on local radio. After that summer replacement show, I became known to 30 to 40 million people who watched that show in the U.S.A., as well as Canada and most English speaking countries in the world.

That TV show and "Everything Is Beautiful," the song I wrote for it, completed my climb up that stairway. That show and that song caused me to be recognized everywhere I went from then on. After that time, I did a lot of things that expanded and secured my popularity, but those were the well-ordered steps that took Ray Ragsdale from Clarkdale, Georgia, to become a performer who played sold out houses everywhere from Sydney, Australia, to London, England, and all over the United States. I say "well ordered," but they were a mystery to me when they were happening. I can only think that a higher power was and is in charge. Thank you, Lord. Amazing Grace.

The Nashville Breakfast Club

Nashville is a multi-cultural, ethnically diverse, dynamic Southern city on the banks of the Cumberland River, nestled in the foothills of the Cumberland Plateau that has many faces. There are all kinds of businesses, from health care, insurance and radio, to printing and recording and on and on. A good example of that diversity is represented by the people with whom I share breakfast every Saturday morning when I am in town. The Nashville Breakfast Club, as some of us call it, includes or has included record industry people, car salesmen, a stock broker, an advertising agency owner, a radio personality, musicians, songwriters, background singers, book authors, a TV icon or two, and even a college professor. Our little group is just one of Nashville's many faces. Here are the members in our little club. I've already introduced some of them during the writing of this book, but there are others.

George "Goober" Lindsay was an actor and comedian who endeared himself to the hearts of millions as a regular on the long-running and highly popular "Andy Griffith

Show" as the hayseed gas station attendant "Goober" Pyle. He was the awkward cousin of Gomer Pyle, played by Jim Nabors. I had the pleasure to know Jim a little, and Ole Goob a lot. I remember picking George up for breakfast one Saturday and, as he approached the car, he said "Oh, I forgot my hat" and turned around and ran back in his house. When he came back out he was wearing a drum major's hat, replete with a tall plume.

We always take turns paying for breakfast and one morning, as George picked up the check for the entire table, he studied it for a long time and then asked, "Who had the jelly?" On another occasion, after having a pretty bad meal at a restaurant on the road, the waitress was hopeful of a rave review so she could brag to others. She asked, "So how did you enjoy your meal?" as Goober paid his bill. He smiled and said, "Ya'll have great salt."

Ralph Emery, radio DJ, TV personality, and best-selling author, is known to millions of country music fans. Ralph had a highly rated television show on TNN (The Nashville Network) for several years. It is amazing when you realize that the current highest rated news show on cable TV, "The O'Reilly Factor" on Fox News Channel, has a huge audience but does not draw the number of viewers who tuned into Ralph Emery and his "Nashville Now" variety/talk show on TNN on a nightly basis for almost ten years.

Ralph exudes that folksy "come on in and sit down and listen to this" persona that only a few media personalities are born with. Ralph is a native Tennessean, and is in good company because the likes of Dinah Shore, Phil Harris, and Pat Boone are all from Tennessee as well.

Norris "Norro" Wilson is a comedian both on and off stage 24 hours a day, as well as a songwriter, record producer, and mighty fine singer. As someone once said, "Norro" is what you get when you let a kid pick his own name. Norro is from Scottsville, Kentucky, about an hour up the road from Nashville, but a million miles away from the music business. Norro and I grew up in Nashville in the music business and have had an association for years, although we have not worked together all that much. He had a lounge act in Vegas for years, co-wrote "The Most Beautiful Girl in the World" for Charlie Rich with Billy Sherrill, and wrote "The Grand Tour" for George Jones, along with numerous other hits. He produced almost all of the number one hits for Charley Pride, in addition to producing records for Eddy Arnold, Tammy Wynette, Shania Twain, Kenny Chesney, and numerous others. Norro is just naturally funny and has inspired me with his humor for years.

Alan "Do-rite" Sullivan is the working girl's best friend, ex-car salesman, current stock broker, bon vivant, and man about town. When you ask Do-rite how he's doing, he is apt to tell you that he is "blooming with pleasure and flowing with achievement and feel so good you couldn't hit me in the ass with a palm leaf fan." Now, I have heard that phrase thousands of times and I still don't know what it means but, loosely translated, I think it is the equivalent of "Fine, thank you. How are you?" Do-rite is my stock broker and has been for years, but he started out in life as a salesman for the only Cadillac dealer in Nashville back in the day. The time was just after World War II, and he had a friend named Hamilton Wallace the Third, or "Hambone" to his friends, of whom I happened to be one. Do-rite and Hambone were, as they say in the South, a "caution." Once, an elderly and rather wealthy Belle Meade lady came to the Cadillac dealership to pick up her new car. When Hambone drove the car around the building, after just having had it washed, the lady said "That's not my car!" Hambone said, "I beg your pardon?!!?" The lady then said, "I ordered a black car and that's not the color black I ordered." Hambone opened his mouth to protest and tell the lady that Cadillac only made one color of black, but Do-rite stepped forward and said, "The lady is absolutely right, Hamilton. Her car is parked behind the building. Would you go get it for her please?"

As Hambone drove slowly around the building, Do-rite apologized to the lady and, when Ham appeared a few minutes later, in the very same car she exclaimed "Now that's my car!" Both Do-rite and Ham agreed, and said they were very sorry for the unfortunate mistake.

If you ever compliment Do-rite on his attire, he will most likely say that he has a hot date and the lady has a sister, if you can get away for an hour or two. He lives and moves in the high society circles of Nashville and once at a society function, he brought what he told everyone was a special pate that he thought they would enjoy. Everyone loved it and wanted to know where they could get it because it was the best pate they had ever had. Do-rite was elusive and never told them that it was actually Vienna Sausages straight from the can, mashed together with a little black pepper.

Bill Hudson is owner and driving force behind Bill Hudson and Associates, an advertising and public relation firm that has served Nashville since 1963, and is Nashville's oldest full service marketing and communications company. Bill has been in audio and video studios for years producing ground breaking commercials, ad campaigns, and events for many Nashville Stars.

Doug Gilmore was a star quarterback at Vanderbilt in the 1950s, played in a college bowl game, and is the writer of two number one songs, one for Jerry Lee Lewis and the other for Reba McEntire. He has been a music consultant on numerous TV shows, like "Sonny and Cher," and the John Denver specials, to mention only a few. In Los Angeles, he worked for the artist management firm that represented me and Roger Miller, along with my long-time friend and one-time manager, Don Williams. Doug currently works occasionally with Morgan Freeman's video and film production operation in Clarksdale, Mississippi," near Memphis.

Don Light came to Nashville from a little town just a few miles north of here to be a drummer and as such he worked his way onto the Grand Ole Opry, where he was a staff drummer for years. Later, he ran the Nashville office for *Billboard* magazine, and then opened the Don Light Talent Agency. Don provided booking for gospel music acts and was so instrumental in the growing success of that genre that he was inducted into the Gospel Music Hall of Fame. He also enabled the careers of Jimmy Buffet and, more recently, Dailey and Vincent. Don has kept a diary for years. He can tell stories with great humor and accuracy. What a book that little diary would make.

Don Cusic is that college professor I mentioned and he helped with this book. He has authored over 25 of his own. He teaches at Belmont University, just off Music Row, and is a music business historian. Among those 20 books are the biographies of Roger Miller, Eddy Arnold, and Gene Autry. Recently he produced a CD of original songs by

Bobby Bare. There's not much that goes on, or has ever gone on down on Music Row, that Don Cusic or Don Light do not know about.

Chet Atkins was probably the founder and charter member of the Breakfast Club. We miss him every day, and especially on Saturday mornings. Chet loved to eat at Cracker Barrel for two reasons: he liked the food, and as a spokesperson for them he always ate for free. Once, when out of town, he invited some guys to go with him to break-fast and they ended up driving over 40 miles just to get to a Cracker Barrel. Gas was cheaper back then and 40 miles for a free breakfast made good sense to my frugal friend.

There are a couple of semi-regulars of the Breakfast Club – Bergen White, and Buddy Kalb. Bergen works the road a fair amount of time, so he is not always in town. Buddy lives in Hendersonville, about 20 miles north of Nashville, so some Saturdays he sleeps in rather than make the 40 minute drive. He won't go as far for breakfast as Chet would.

Bergen is an arranger and vocalist who, like me, substi-tuted for different members of the Jordanaires from time to time. He is a much in-demand session arranger who has written and directed shows for Elvis, Garth Brooks, Martina McBride, and others. You may remember an album he produced that was a classic, *For Women Only,* or be intrigued to know that he was part of the rock group Ronny and the Daytonas, who had the hit "G.T.O." Bergen has had an illustrious career in the Nashville recording industry, but his great hidden talent is that he can hit a golf ball further and straighter than anybody I know who isn't on the PGA Tour. Whenever I get asked to provide a foursome for some celebrity golf outing, Bergen is my first call. Lately, he has been working on a Christmas Album for the Robertson Family of Duck Dynasty fame.

C. W. "Buddy" Kalb is my songwriting friend from way back in my Atlanta days. Buddy gave up on the music business for a few years after he couldn't get any traction as Big Buddy K, and concentrated on his "day job" at Ford Motor Company, where he did very well, but he never gave up on writing. He has written lots of songs for me to record, and many more for my music publishing companies. We write together from time to time, but usually we don't do it sitting together face to face. I used to say that Buddy and I went to different high schools together, me at Druid Hills and him at Decatur, an adjoining Atlanta area community. That's sort of how we co-write; he does his thing, gives me what he's come up with, and then I do mine or vice versa. It's different, but it works.

Others come and go from time to time, and a few, like Goober and Chet, have passed on, as has Wayne Sharpe, who was a used car salesman. Wayne worked for Barry Smith, who was also a regular, and owned Music City Motors, which specialized in exotic cars for country music stars. If a country music star could dream of a car he or she wanted, then Barry would find it – from a Ferrari to a one of a kind luxury motor home, or even a yacht. If you had the dream and the money, then Barry could make that motorized dream come true for you. Barry and his wife, Sheri, sang and opened the show for George Jones for years after Barry recorded a song and George heard him sing it. The song was "Mama Used to Whup Me With a George Jones Album, That's Why I Sing This Way." Sheri still works on the road with me as one of my background singers and reluctant faux-fiddle player, and appears in some of my videos. She was the girl who carried the Round Number Card in "The Blue Cyclone," and Barry was my "good Buddy Bill" in that video.

Two others who are no longer with us are "Slick" Lawson, and Houston "Hootie" Thomas, both of whom were great cooks. Houston opened restaurants around town; the last one was Sperry's, which is now run by his son, Allison. Slick was a musician and photographer who did freelance work for *People* magazine, as well as many of my album covers down through the years. Slick's specialty in the kitchen was gumbo.

Slick and Do-rite were balloonists and, on one occasion, they descended and landed in a place way back in the country. They sat in a local bar as they waited for the pick-up van to locate them and load the balloon and basket. They were nervously concerned about the rough crowd that continually eyed the city strangers in their colorful ballooning attire. When Slick saw the van pull up outside with all their equipment already on board, he rose and stepped to the middle of the barroom floor and asked, "Who's the meanest S.O.B in this place?" A deep hush fell over the entire bar until a chair loudly scraped the floor and broke the tense silence. A large, Grizzly Adams-looking character stood up and said "I reckon that'd be me." Slick then said, "Good, I gotta leave now and I'm puttin' you in charge." The entire bar then erupted in laughter. Do-rite was already out the door and headed for the van as Slick finished his speech, but Slick got there before Do-rite and, as they said on "Hee Haw," – PFFT they were gone!

I love my Saturday morning gatherings and sharing coffee and stories with the Nashville Breakfast Club. I love Nashville with the "Meat and Three" restaurants serving home cooked meals where the waitresses all call you 'Honey' and where you can be a recognized Music Business celebrity while the folks just smile and say "Howdy" and let you enjoy your breakfast, lunch or dinner. I love the casual relaxed atmosphere and the moderate climate, not too hot and not too cold, but just right.

The Nashville that many people dream of and want to visit is actually a myth. Folks from all over the country come expecting something created in their imagination as they listen to the Grand Ole Opry or watch a TV Show like "Nashville" or listen to their favorite star's latest record. Perhaps, in their minds, they put themselves up on that legendary stage or they imagine themselves running into stars on the street, or being able to walk into a record company and give a star the hit song they have written. The facts are quite different. It can be a hard-luck town for many with dreams of instant stardom and a destination of disappointment that can't possibly live up to folks' exaggerated expectations.

For me, Nashville was and is all I ever dreamed it would be – and far more. Ray Stevens' Nashville is a quilt of great relationships and experiences that are uniquely mine. I love Nashville, and I'm going to keep on exploring all that she is and all that she has for me. I hope you have enjoyed hearing about my journey, where and how I started, and how I have landed. Come see me whenever I'm in your town, or the next time you are in mine, and bring along this book. I'd love to meet you and sign it for you.

Look at the most prominent animal on that ball...it's Clyde. This could be an episode for the Twilight Zone.

Little Ray, Happy Happy Happy.

Four generations from left – my dad, his dad, and great granddad holding me.

Mama and Me in a photo booth at the Carnival near Clarkdale.

My last school picture in Clarkdale.

AHS
Class of '57
Ray
Ragsdale
Stevens

My name tag from my 50th class reunion at Albany High School.

My Dad on the left – he was the Clarkdale MVP – with co-MVP Bully Coalson on the right.

The Clarkdale Baseball Team in 1948.

Penny and Me making funny faces at a New Year's Eve party at our house.

My beautiful girls... Suzi and Timi.

Penny and Me in Washington.

Norro Wilson, Chet Atkins, Me, Jerry Reed, Bob Beckham, and Harry Warner...The Possum Pack.

A Tommy Roe session at Rick Hall's Fame Studios in Muscle Shoals (Standing from left: Rick Hall, Felton Jarvis, Tommy Roe, Me, David Briggs, and Norbert Putnam; seated at bottom left: Jerry Carrigan.

Kneeling from left: Bill Justis, Charlie McCoy, Buddy Harman, Me, Louis Nunley. First row standing: Shelby Singleton, Dave Dryer, Minna Dryer, Delores Denning, Brook Benton standing behind young Sidney Singleton, Margie Singleton, Dottie Dillard, Boots Randolph. Second row standing: Mort Thomason, Pig Robbins, Charlie Bradley, Gil Wright peering over Minna's head, Kelso Hearston standing next to Brook. Back row: Harold Bradley, Selby Coffeen, Ed Grizzard, Jerry Kennedy, and Bob Moore.

Shelby Singleton looks on as I ran down "Ahab the Arab" during that day we recorded three big hits.

A publicity picture during the Ray Stevens NBC Summer Show Era.

Roger Miller (he even held his glass funny), Shelby Singleton, and Me at a BMI Awards party.

A float trip down the Buffalo River with a bunch of guys who are a lot older now. Can you find me? (From left: unknown, Buzz Cason, Tommy Alsup, unknown, Mike Shepherd, me, unknown, Harry Warner, Hubert Long, and Norro Wilson.)

*Penny and I in
Washington, D.C.
for the Nixon
inauguration.*

*Ed Cramer gives me a BMI performance award for "Everything is
Beautiful" as Mike Shepherd looks on.*

Here am I with Dusty Springfield and Andy Williams during an appearance on his television show. In the lower left hand corner you'll see a very young Donny Osmond partially pictured.

Penny and I are at a BMI dinner in Nashville.

Here I am on the left with (l to r) Penny, Margaret Ann and Harry Warner with Atlanta publisher Bill Lowery.

My former manager Don Williams, Penny, and me kissing Grace Gallico, wife of publisher Al Gallico, and, partially pictured on far right, Patsy Wilson, wife of Norro.

Me and my girls at Big Cedar Lodge just outside Branson, MO.

From left to right is Penny, Frances Preston (then head of the Nashville office of BMI), me, Don Williams, and Ed Cramer, who was President of BMI.

Album cover for Ray Stevens Greatest Hits Vol. II. Norro is the umpire.

The Nashville Breakfast Club – Houston Thomas, Barry Smith, Norro Wilson, Me, Harry Warner, Goober, Wayne Sharpe, and Do-rite Sullivan.

The Nashville Breakfast Club – Norro Wilson, Me, Harry Warner, Goober, and Wayne Sharpe.

The Itty Bitty Squirt Band (From Left – Brother John, Norro Wilson, Buddy Kalb, Randy Cullers on drums, standing is Doug Gilmore, Me, Larry McFaden, a dancer whose name I can't remember, and Melanie Greenwood).

Loretta Lynn, Ray Charles, and Me.

Left to right: Harry Warner, Jimmy Dean, Chet Atkins, Don Light, and me.

Meeting President Reagan and Nancy (From Left – barely seen Richard Sterban of the Oak Ridge Boys, Me, Bill Monroe, and Anne Murray.

Backstage at the Desert Inn in Las Vegas where Louise Mandrell and I were performing (From left: Barbara Mandrell, Jim Stephany, Don Williams, Me, and Louise.

Don Williams and Me on the shoot of "Santa Claus is Watching You" video in Hollywood.

There's Chet in my office – Bill Carlisle told him he was a "Turable" fiddle player, but he kept at it.

Backstage with Faron Young, Kris Kristofferson, and his road manager.

*My folks and
me in Branson
– 1993.*

*Me, Penny,
and the girls
at a party at
Suzi's condo.*

*The grandbabes
– Hayden
holding Willis,
with Emma
right, and 'lil
Aubrey left.*

Me and Ole Bud during the Christmas Shows at the Acuff Theatre here in Nashville.

My brother John as M.C. of the Ray Stevens Show.

On an awards show with Tammy Wynette.

*On the air with
Ralph Emery
discussing the
possum casserole I
brought him.*

*Don Williams
at the Pancake
Pantry, just off
Music Row.*

*The two best
guitar players
I ever heard –
Jerry Reed and
Chet Atkins.*

Harry and Bonnie Warner with me at Opryland in Nashville.

One of the many drawings Randy Cullers has done over the years of life in the Ray Stevens band on the road.

Recording at my first studio.

*Dad, Mom, Me,
Bill Lowery, and
Sam Wilhoit.*

On the Fox News set with
Sean Hannity.

Old Goob – George Lindsay –
and Me.

The old man on the
red carpet at the CMA
Awards circa 2007.

The Jordanaires
and I dressed to do
"I Saw Elvis In A
UFO." From left –
Gordon Stoker, Neal
Matthews, Me, Louis
Nunley, and Ray
Walker.

Guess who?

Headquarters of the Ray Stevens worldwide, far flung empire.

A

B

R

S

V

W

Made in the USA
Lexington, KY
24 July 2014